ZenAnimals

How to draw zendoodle animals

By Veronica Kim

Contents

Disclaimer

While all attempts have been made to verify the information provided in this book, the author doesn't assume any responsibility for errors, omissions, or contrary interpretations of the subject matter contained within. **The information provided in this book is for educational and entertainment purposes only. The reader is responsible for his or her own actions and the author does not accept any responsibilities for any liabilities or damages, real or perceived, resulting from the use of this information.**

The trademarks that are used are without any consent, and the publication of the trademark is without permission or backing by the trademark owner. All trademarks and brands within this book are for clarifying purposes only and are the owned by the owners themselves, not affiliated with this document.

So you don't think you can draw...

Zendoodle method is a new form of freeform drawing that anyone can do. It does not require any special classes, equipment, or technology. It's simple, relaxing, and best of all, anyone can pick up a pencil and a piece of paper and do it.

This book will start you with the basics, and, in no time you'll be drawing Zendoodle animals like a pro.

Introduction

Zendoodle method is the process of drawing patterns within a framework. Anything from simple boxes to animals can be drawn using this technique, and this eBook will show you:

- What Zendoodle Drawing is

- What you need to draw them

- How to get started

- How to get into more complex shapes

- When to do them

Chapter 1: What is Zen doodle Method?

It is the art of free-hand, free-flowing meditative drawing. It has no specific rules or guidelines. There are no special tools or papers. Just think of all the times you've been on the phone and let your pen or pencil scribble and doodle as you spoke to someone or waited on hold. It's a little like that.

It's a form of abstract drawing. It does not look like anything in particular. It doesn't have to be. It is free-flowing and doesn't have an ordered form. It is a representation of letting your hand mindlessly draw on the page. It can be started at any angle and finish at angle. The basic shape can be many different forms. It's what is inside the main form that is the focus of this artful technique.

There is no set angle to view these pieces of work from either. Being completely abstract, every angle you view it from can give you new impressions and new things to find in zendoodle pictures. You'll surprise yourself at what you can create.

It does not take years of art classes to get started. All it takes is letting your mind go and your hand to move free across the paper, making patterns within patterns.

Most zendoodle drawings, if not all of them, are black and white, which can give them depth, but you can use color in them as well to bring more dimension to your works.

Some only take about fifteen minutes to draw and can be drawn on small squares of paper. As you get more comfortable, try larger patterns and pieces of paper. If you want to mix it up, try different colors of paper and ink.

What's the difference between Zendoodle method and Doodling?

This is a common question when first learning this technique.

Doodling is often done out of boredom with no particular rhyme or reason. Your mind wanders and takes over your hand, putting it on auto, filling margins with scribbles, lines, circles, and whatever else pops into your head. It's not intended to be any sort of art in any way. It's just your mind trying to stay alert during the tedium of listening to a long lecture or being put on hold for what seems like an eternity.

Zendoodle art is mindful and more focused. It is filling a frame with patterns and designs in order to make a composition. It is meditative concentration on what is in front of you. Your mind is focused on nothing but the paper, the empty frame, and the pencil in your hand. It is concentrating on what patterns to place where in order to make the composition jump off of the page and grab attention when it is finished. It is an art form.

Chapter 2: What do I need?

The thing about zendoodle drawings is the fact that you don't need any specialized items to make the works of art.

Pencils

Unlike sketching and drawing portraiture, any pencil from mechanical to a traditional No.2 standard will work fine.

Pencil Sharpener

You're only going to need this if you are using traditional pencils.

Felt tip pens

Fine tip pens to ink in your drawings are needed, but they don't have to be high-end. You can use a very fine or fine sharpie marker for this.

Paper

Drawing grade paper is perfect for zendoodle art, but you can also use heavy weight printer paper as well. If you like inking your creations make sure the paper is thick enough not to bleed through.

Nice Quite Spot

Yep, you need to find a relaxing and quiet place to let your mind relax and the ideas flow freely. This is a form of meditation; so, being aware of your breathing and letting your mind be devoid of all the day's stresses will make it more enjoyable.

Music

This is optional, but relaxing music, like smooth jazz or meditative music, can help relax the spirit and mind.

Clearing your mind

Like mindful and meditative techniques, your mind must be free and clear of all the day's worries. Just close your eyes for a moment and think of relaxing places and thoughts. This will put you in the right frame of mind.

Chapter 3: In the beginning...

You have your materials, your mind is focused and ready, and now you are wondering where to start. You've looked online and seen all the wondrous creations done with this technique and your mind is reeling about how to get started and if you can even do this. You can. You just need to start at the beginning.

Let's start with a simple square:

As you can see, the square doesn't have to be one made with a ruler. The lines don't even have to be straight. It's a simple little square that is begging to be filled with patterns. We're going to do a wave to start.

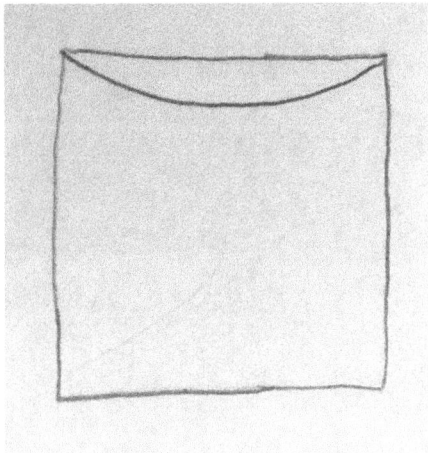

Draw it like the one in the picture above. It only

needs to be from corner to corner. Now draw more

like rays going across, like in the next picture.

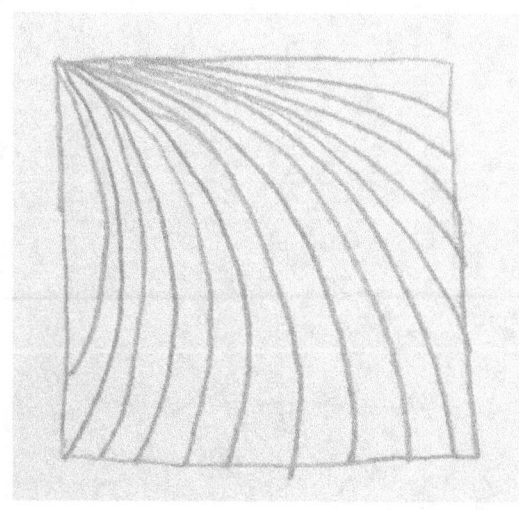

This is the same picture. We have just turned it so
the rays look like they are coming toward you. With
this art form, you can orient the picture any way you
please. We've got the basic pattern. Now all we need
to do is add a little more.

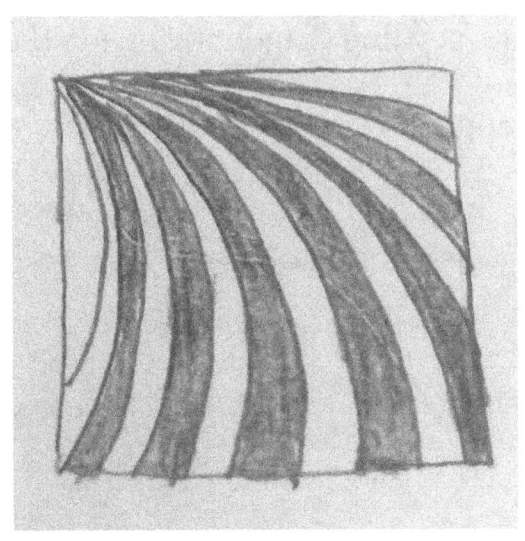

Color in almost every other line, and you've got your first Zendoodle picture. Now, draw another basic square. We're going to do something different. It's going to be a little more intricate, but not overly so.

Let's draw a wavy line diagonally inside the square.
Just let it happen. It doesn't have to be exactly like
the picture. Just a wavy line in the shape will be just
fine.

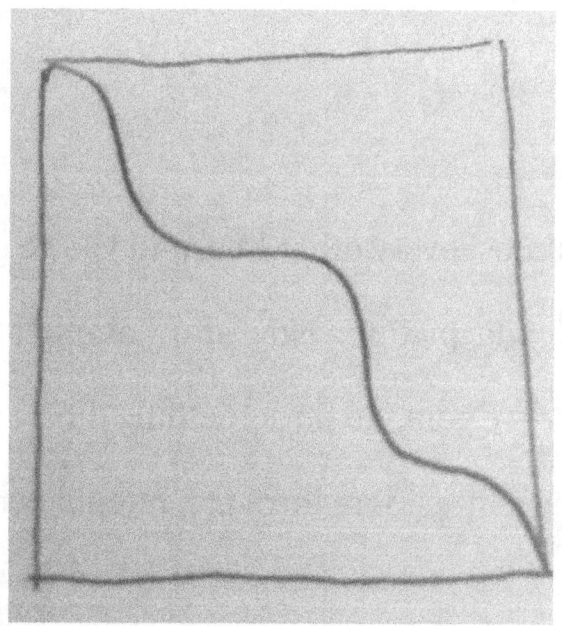

Repeat your wavy line all the way to the top right
corner. Don't fill in the bottom yet. We are going to
fill it in a different way. The lines can be as close or
far apart as you feel. Since this is abstract, always
keep in mind that the end result is up to you. There
isn't a wrong or right way. These are just general
guides.

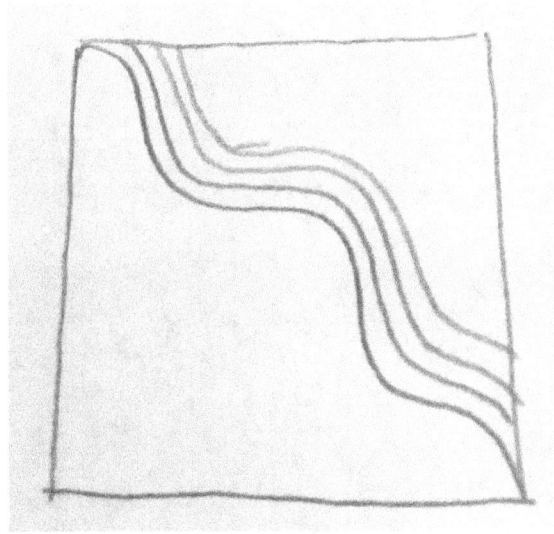

We are going to give it a different dimensional for the bottom half. Remember those waves from the first square? Add them here to the bottom half of the square. Don't fill them in like you did before.

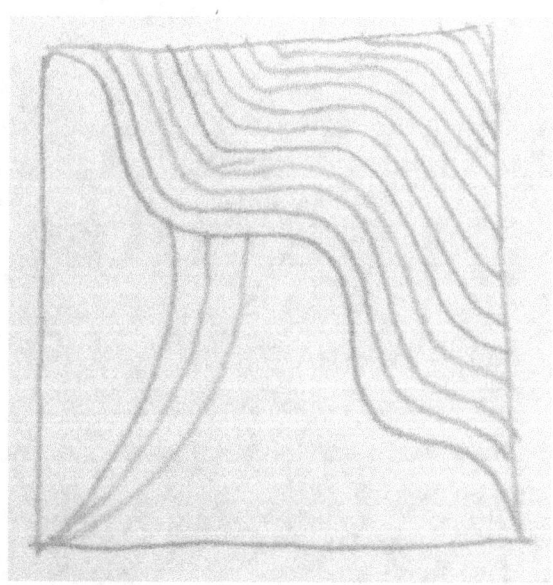

Your picture should look like this at this stage.

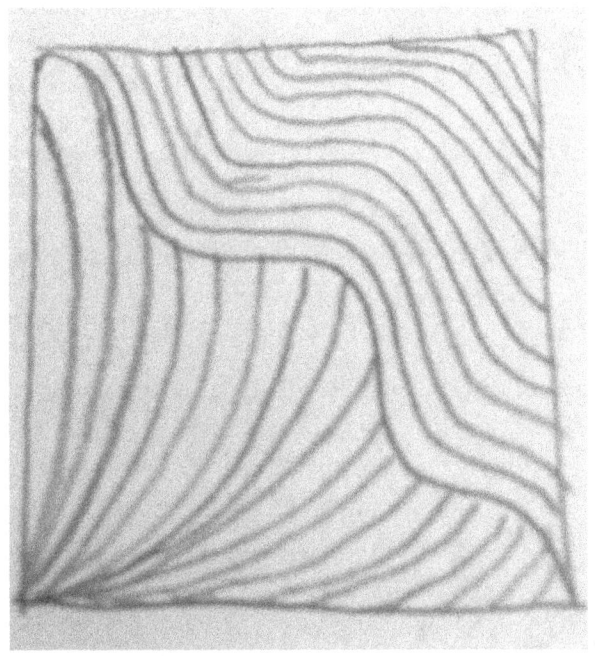

You are now going to fill in the spaces on the bottom half in a couple of different ways to illustrate how you can vary patterns within the pattern.

Here we have the progression as it happens:

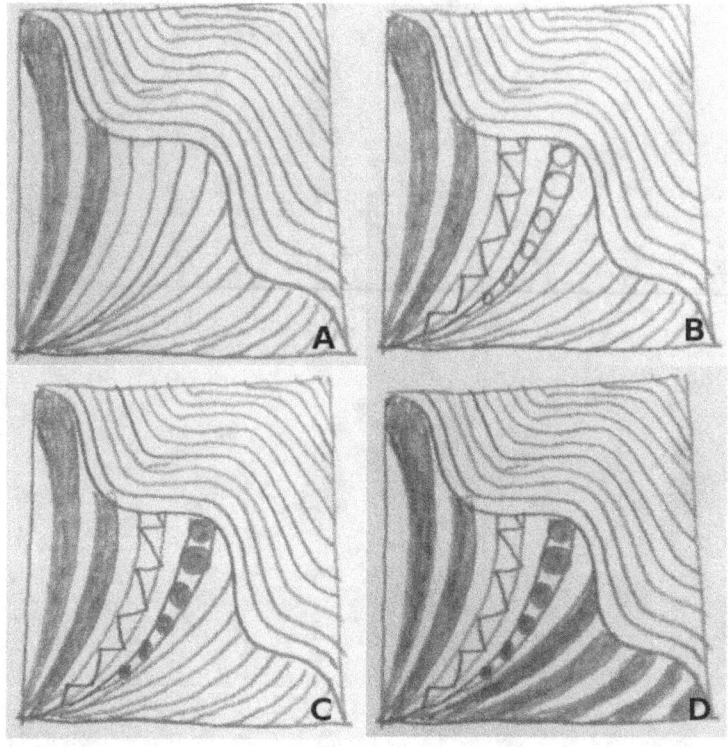

A. We shade in the second and fourth sections like we did the first square.

B. Then draw zig-zags into the next one, and add circles to the one two over.

C. Now, we fill in the circles.

D. The last few are shaded like the first two.

You have now done one that's a little trickier. Now, we're going to change the frame shape of the drawing. Think paisley.

Draw a simple curved raindrop like the one below:

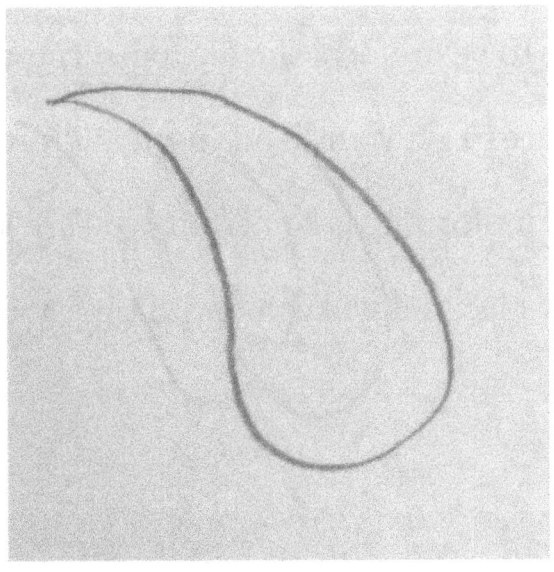

In the next few steps, we are going to embellish the outside as well as the inside. Zendoodle method is not limited to just the inside of the frame. The outside can be decorated as well. It's all according to how you are feeling about which way it should go in terms of the flow of the piece.

Now, draw little bumps all around the outside. They don't have to be uniform starting out. These exercises are to get your hands used to drawing the shapes. If uniformity is something you are looking for in later pieces, it will come with time and practice.

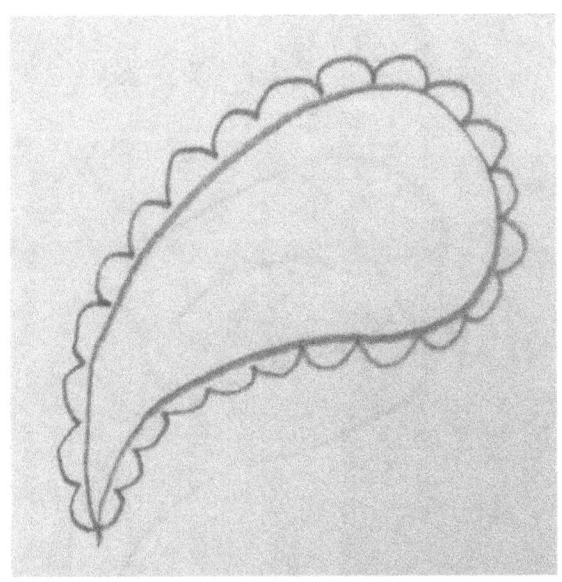

Now, we're going to trace the shape on the inside a few times. This is going to give us a little depth to the piece and more opportunities to fill it in later:

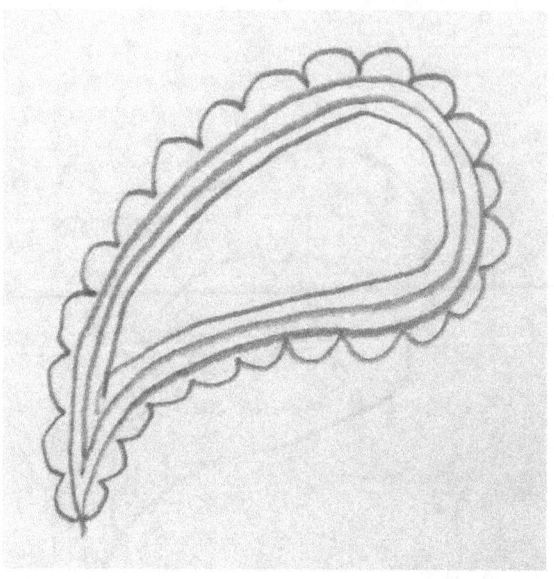

Draw bumps on the inside and then add another tear

in the center. We've some shapes to play with now.

We need to make it stand out a little:

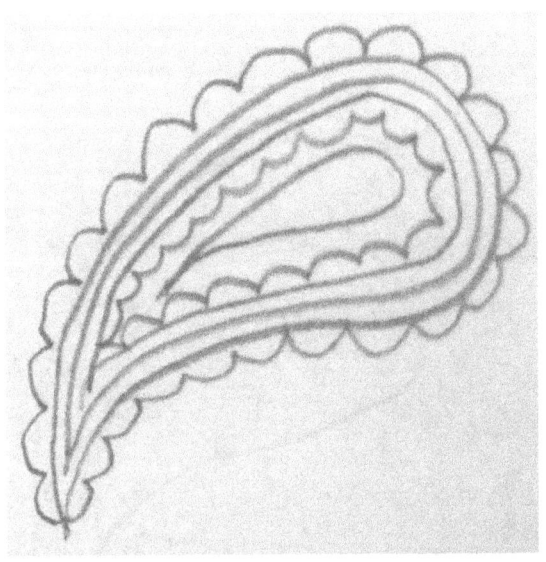

Shade in the middle and then we are going to shade in a few other places. Just one more thing and we will be done with this piece.

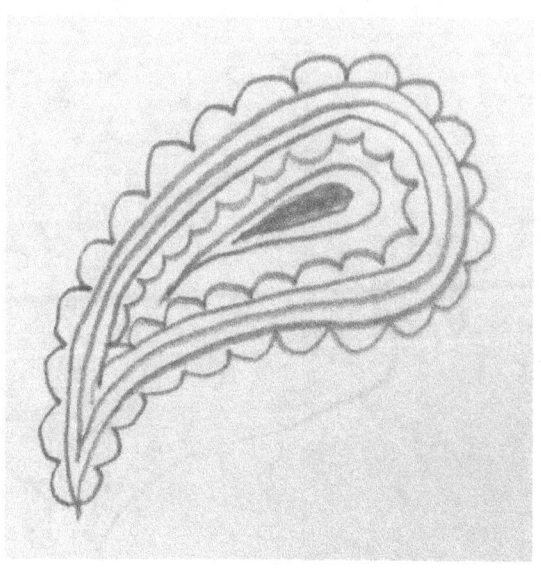

There, now you have done a tear drop. Notice how we reoriented it? If it looks better you the way was oriented before, you can tilt it back. This is about flow and how you feel about the piece.

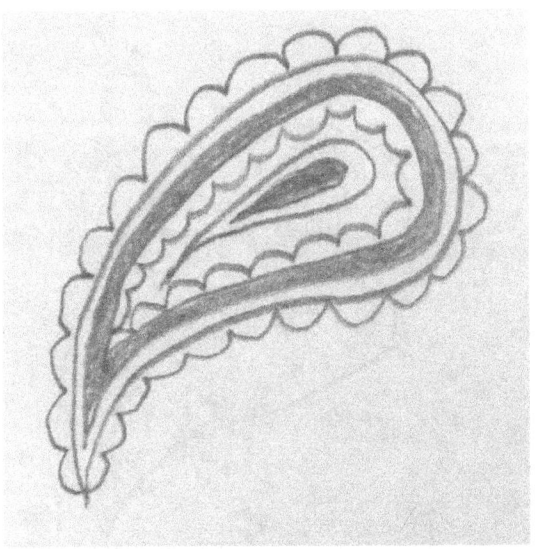

Okay, so we've done simple shapes, let's take the shapes to a slightly more challenging level, but keep the embellishments simple. Start with a basic flower:

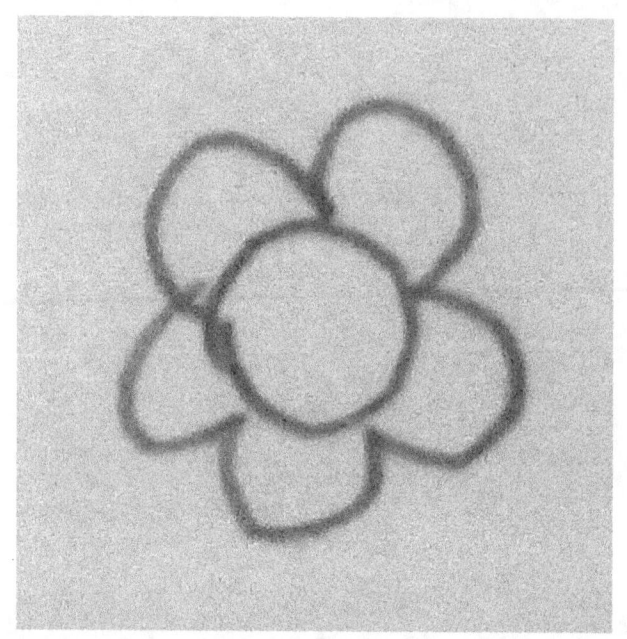

Now, add a layer to it like this:

See how we took the next layer and drew it from the center of one petal to the center of the others? Now, it looks like there are leaves. Let's add a couple more layers the same way to see what happens:

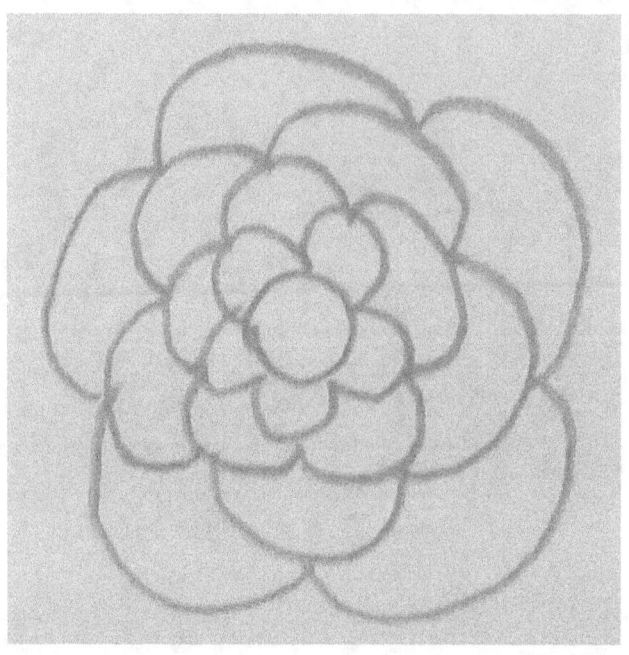

Now we have added the illusion of depth to the

picture, but again, we are not finished. We need to

shade some of it in to finish what we've started:

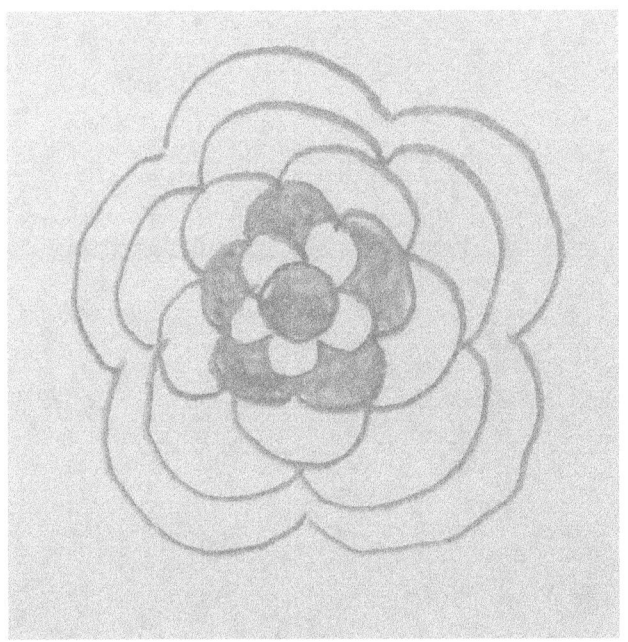

We've still kept it simple, but if you wish to add more,

go right ahead.

Chapter 4: The Fish

Now that you have the basic idea, I am going to increase the difficulty but, not too much. We are going to do an exercise with a simple fish drawing and turn it into something beautiful. This exercise will teach you how much embellishment can be placed in a small frame and still be nice for the eye to look at.

First, draw a basic fish frame like you did when you were small:

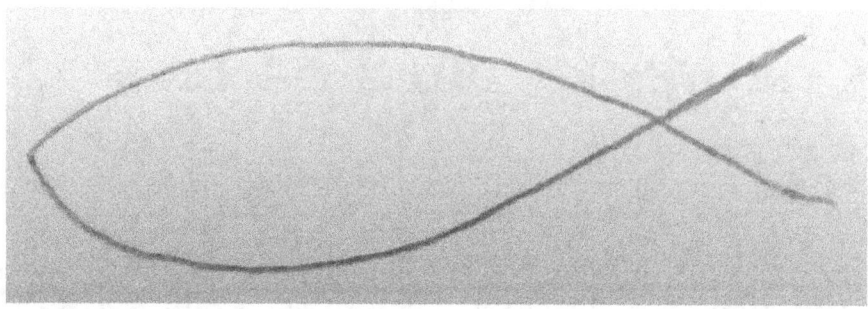

Now, draw one line to separate the head from the body and only add three lines of scales. This is pretty easy.

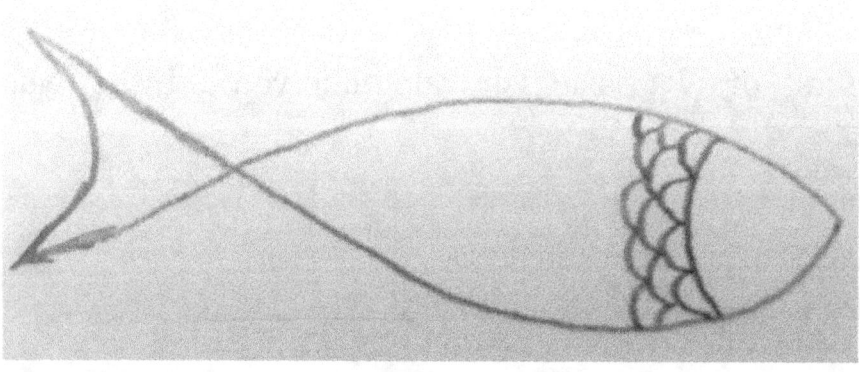

Add loose wavy lines behind the scales. Four lines of these should do it.

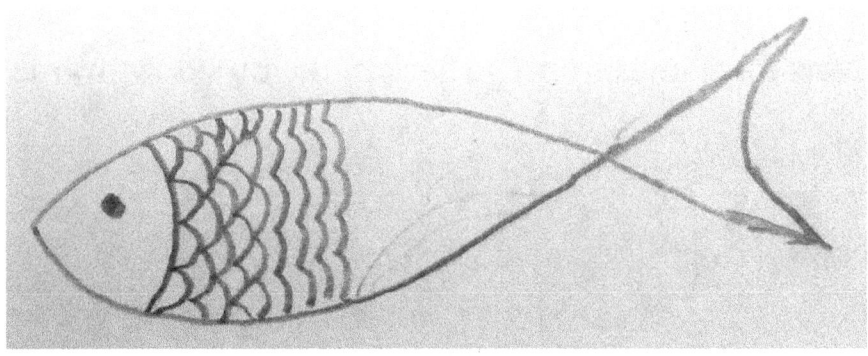

Now, from the top of the drawing, draw eight rays from the second bump down on the wavy line.

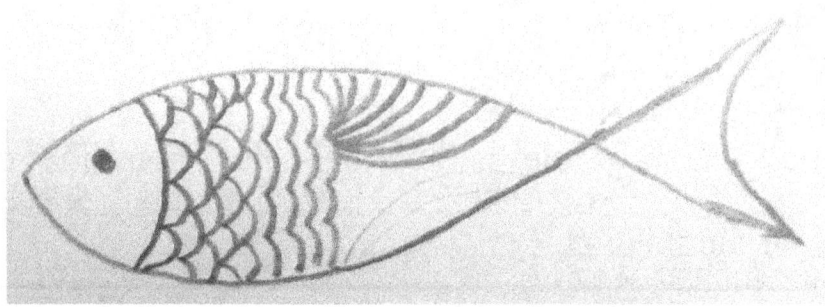

Now wavy lines from the back of the rays downwards, like below:

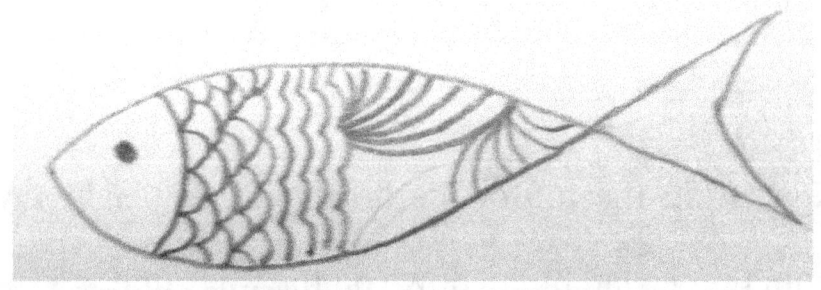

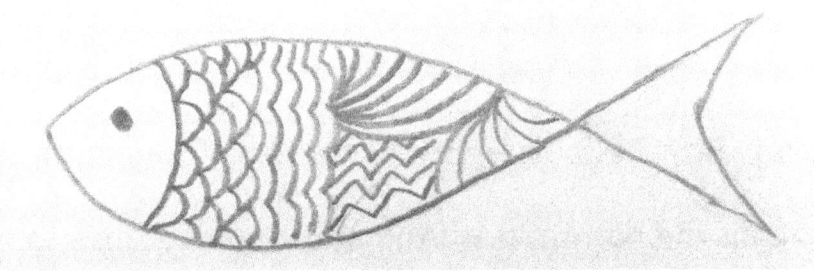

In the space that is left on the body, draw zig-zag lines, like the ones above. Okay. We have the shape and are filling the body, but this fish is still missing a couple of things. We need to draw some fins:

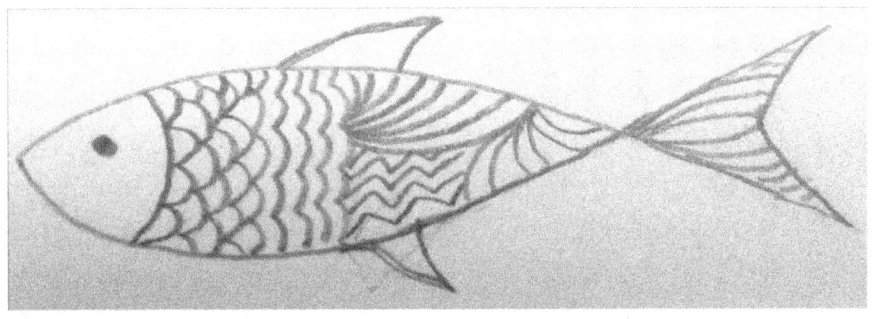

Okay, now he looks more like a fish. Double up the line on the bottom fin. And add rounded lines to his tail. This is filling in nicely, don't you think?

Next, we have to fill in the fins:

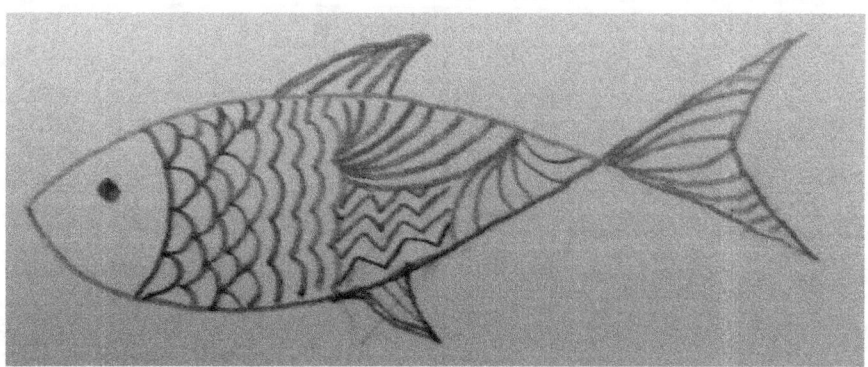

Isn't looking good? We're not done yet. Now, we need to play around with his face a bit. Remember those flowers from above? Let's add some around his eye.

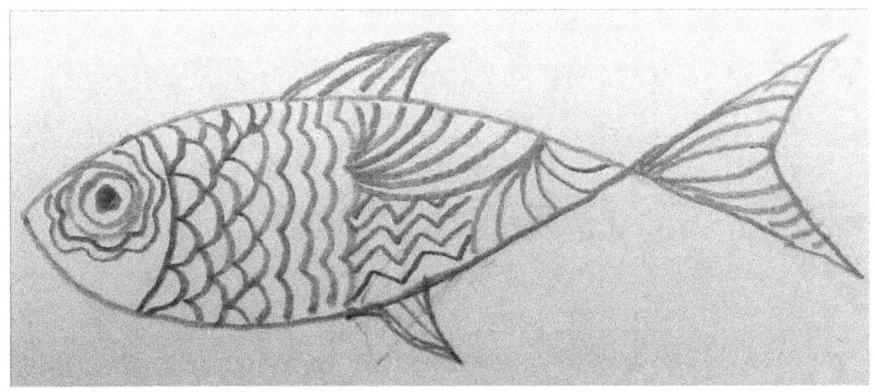

Now, a mouth and just a few lines around his mouth area, like so:

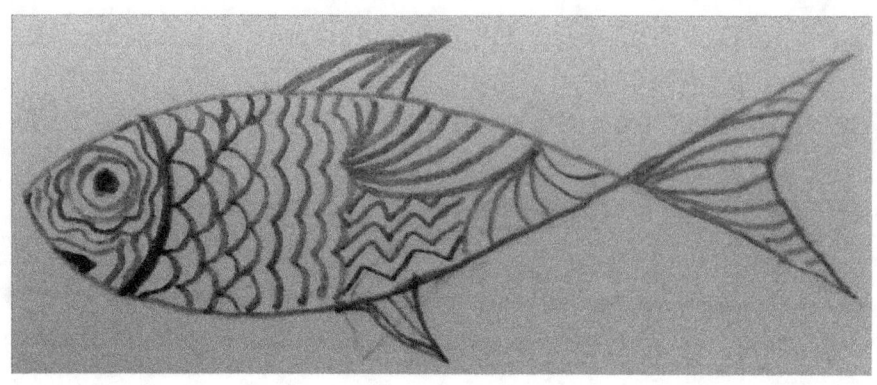

We're on a roll, but we need to add a little more:

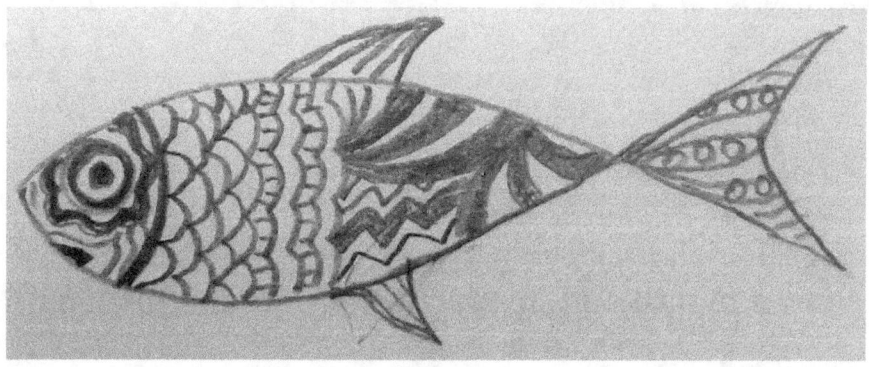

From the front to the back, shade in one ring of flowers around the eye, add closely spaced lines around the waves after the scales, fill in every other ray, one zig-zag, and add circles to the tail. Now, you have a beautiful fish.

If you want to experiment with color, go right ahead. All you would have to do is follow the same instructions for the fish and add colors as you feel and where you're comfortable with adding it. There is no limit.

Chapter 5: The Bird

I know you read the name of the chapter and have your doubts. The basic framework of the bird is all that we are going to draw, and then we will fill it in with all sorts of patterns. This is where you can let your mind focus and go with the flow.

When you start drawing zendoodle animals and even people, you are just drawing the outline of the object you are going to decorate with squiggles, swirls, dots and anything else your mind feels is appropriate.

Always keep in mind that this art form is free-form, abstract. There is no right way or wrong way to fill in a frame. You don't even have to fill in the entire frame. It's all according the way you feel about the composition as a whole.

First, take your paper and draw two large parentheses. Elongate them so they look like the picture below:

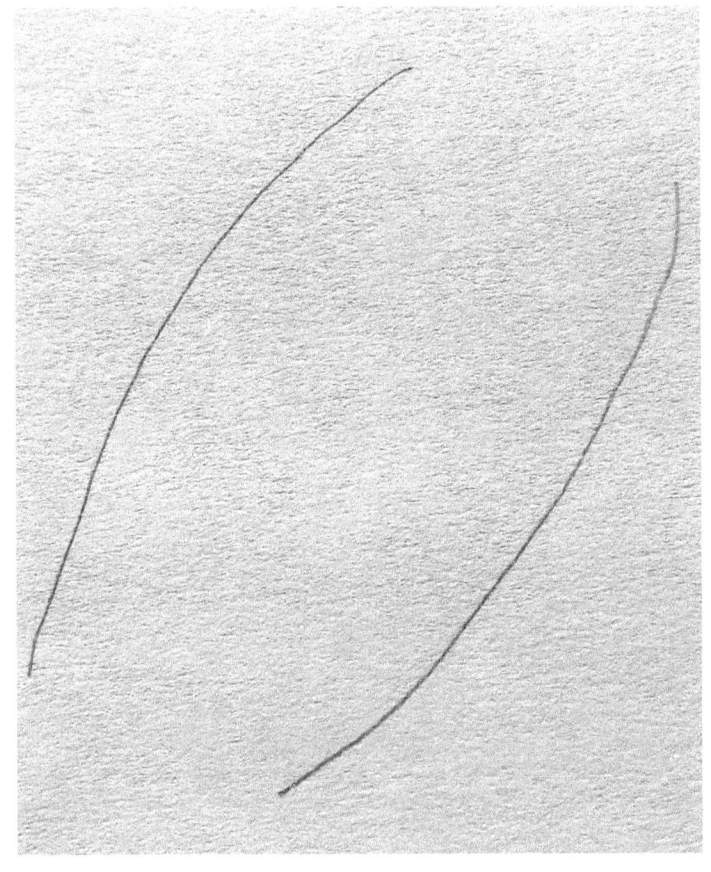

Now, turn the page so the beginning figure is at an angle, and then add a rough sketch of a tail, two curves, and an open circle for the head. It should look like this picture:

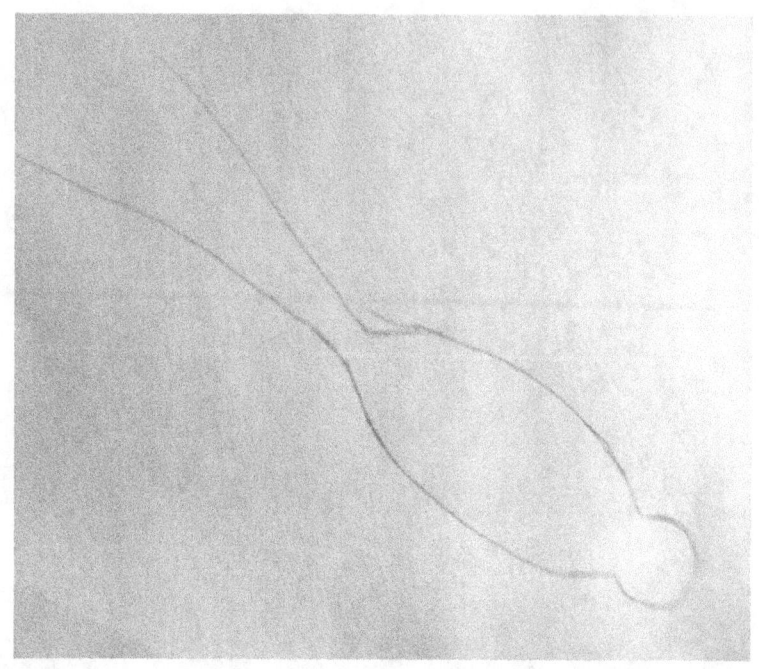

Next, we are going to add the wings:

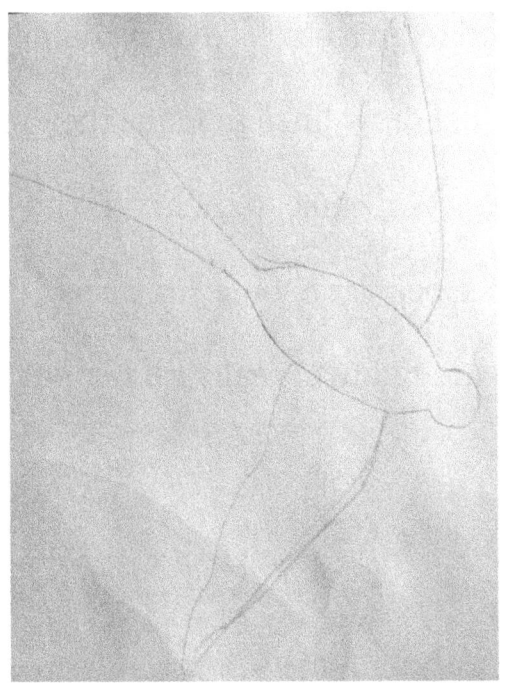

Just think of the wings as arcs with wavy lines under them coming to an end at the main body of the bird. Most of us think about the whole picture, but just focusing on the shapes that make up the figure makes it easier to draw the figure.It's coming together nicely.

Now, we need to give our bird a few details, not many right now. Just draw lines to make the tail and the head feathers. You can cap them off with the small circles you see below or something else. Draw a beak, and now we are ready to really fill her out.

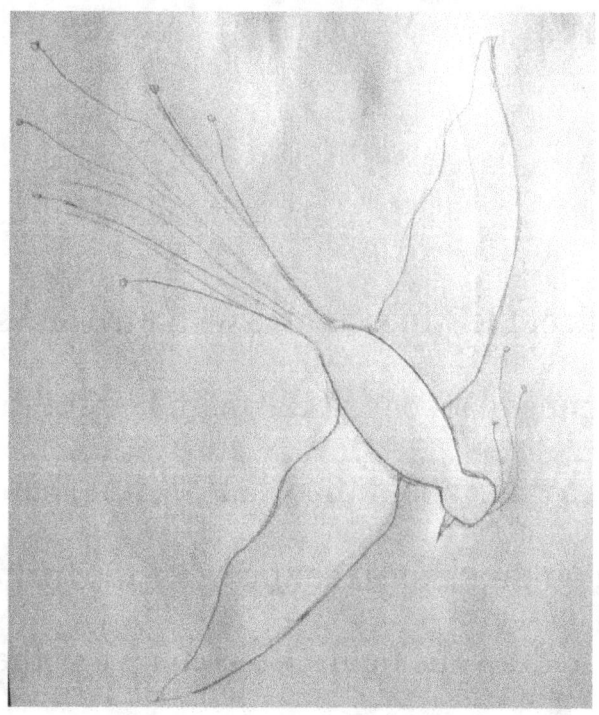

First, draw lines cutting the wings in half. Then, draw rays as you see them in the picture to the left. The bigger the frame, the more you can do with it, but also keep in mind, too much and the eye will try to focus on everything at once and the piece will look too busy to the eye.

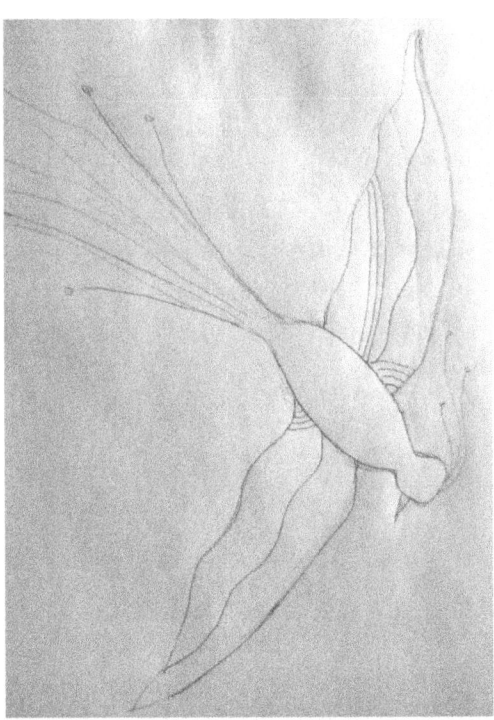

With this size of a project, fill in as you go. It will give your mind a better idea of it wants to do next. Here, we have filled in the rays on the right with shading, and, we have drawn bubbles in the rays on the left. We are working solely on the top of the wings in this picture:

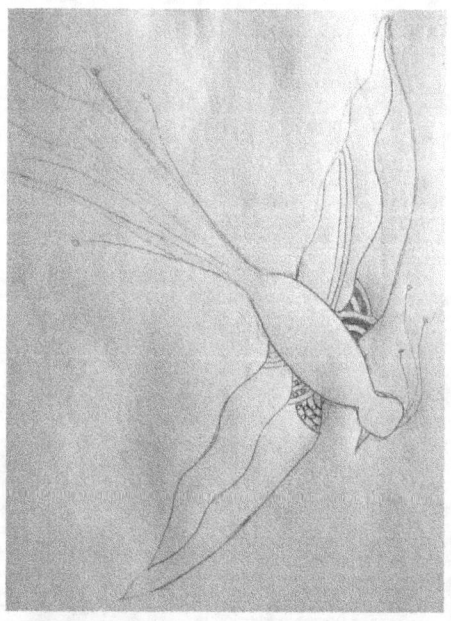

I have turned the picture to help you see the details without me having to devote one page for each example. On the bottom left half of the wing, we have made short lines within the last two rays, and we have added wavy lines, more straight lines with bubbles, and other details.

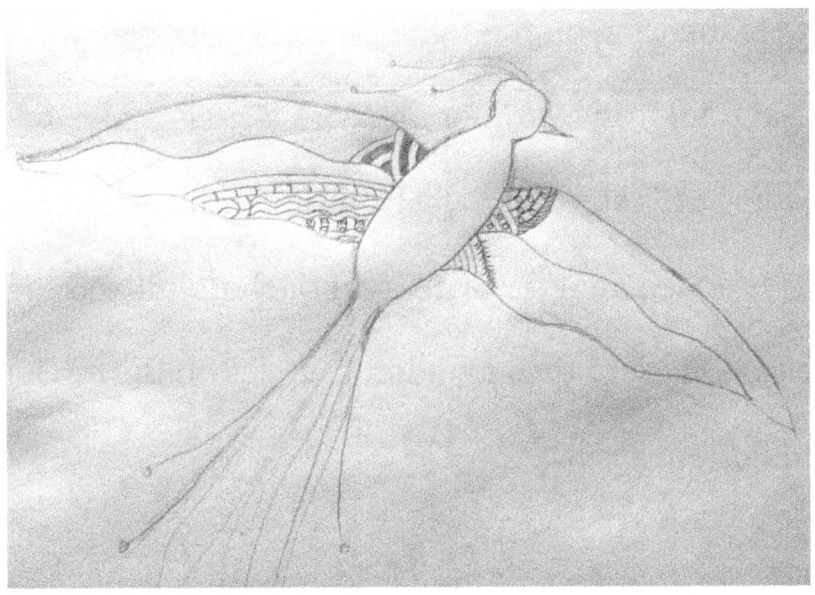

On the bottom right, we have added the sketch of a feather above the rays that were already there. On the top right, we have added another ray and filled it in to look like a rope by drawing in short lines at an angle.

We are beginning to go with the flow of the bisecting line of the wing on the right. Add the triangles you see and fill in every other one with a circle and shading. It's starting to feel a little southwestern. We've added another feather on the bottom, and then we went back to the left, adding circles on the top half and bottom as well.

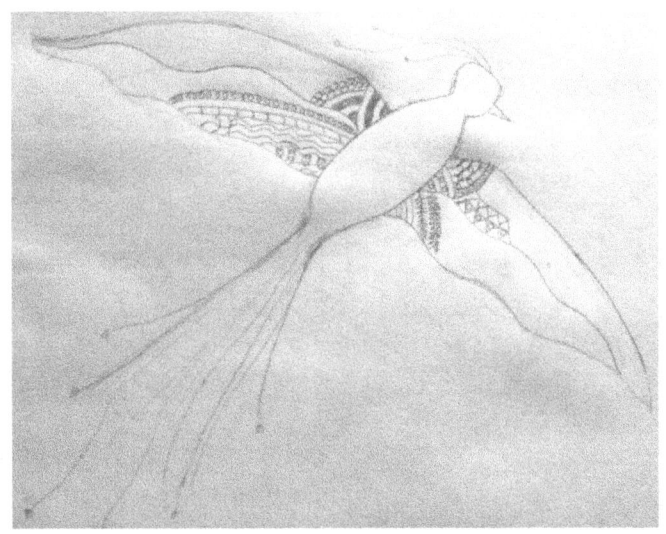

This is where the abstract really begins to shine.
Focusing on the right side, draw concentric circles
and fill them in as you see them in the picture. Now,
make wavy lines on the bottom right until they are
just past the feathers.

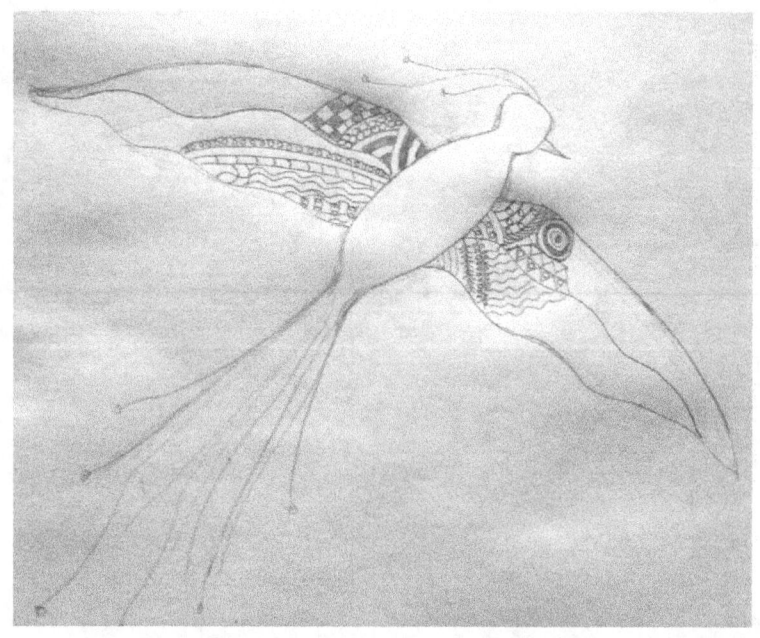

On the left, loosely draw checker squares and fill them in to make them pop. Zendoodle method is not only about filling in patterns. It's also about making the piece eye-catching and something to be admired. You must be happy with the piece and proud of what you create.

Starting with the left this time, draw curves from the innermost part of the design to about the middle. Now, Zig-zag your way to the end of the design as you see in the illustration. Within the wavy lines on the right, draw squiggles in the waves.

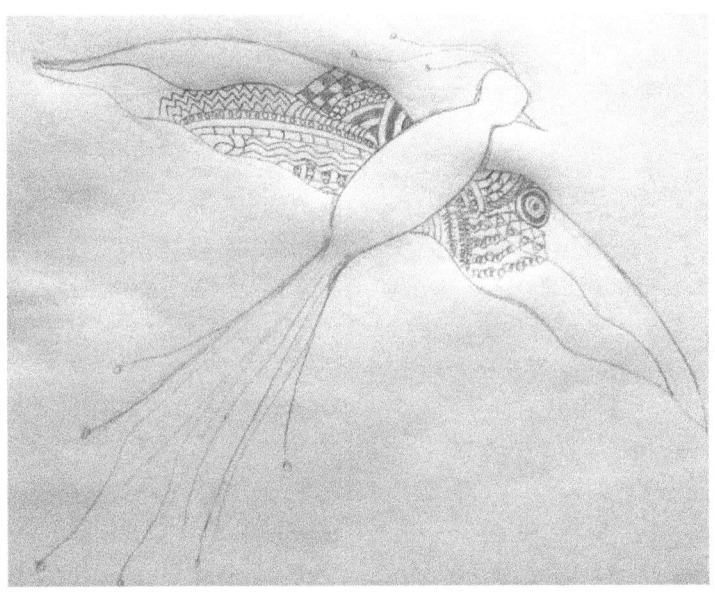

We continue to fill in the wings with four pointed stars, circles, and shaded orbs on the bottom left. We draw in triangles along the bottom edge of the right wing, filling in the bottom row of triangles. We draw shaded diamonds, zig-zags with circles on the ends, and a vine on the top right.

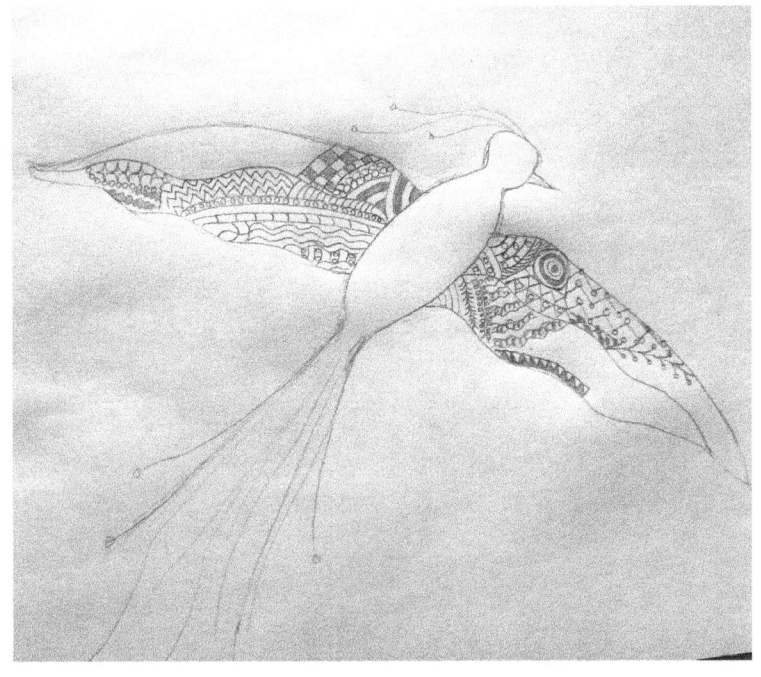

As you can see, we went with the flow of the piece and finished the upper/left wing of the bird. We have a circle with rectangles within it. We have short lines inside the circle. We've added dots, and other designs on the wing as well to add more detail and really make it pop out from the page.

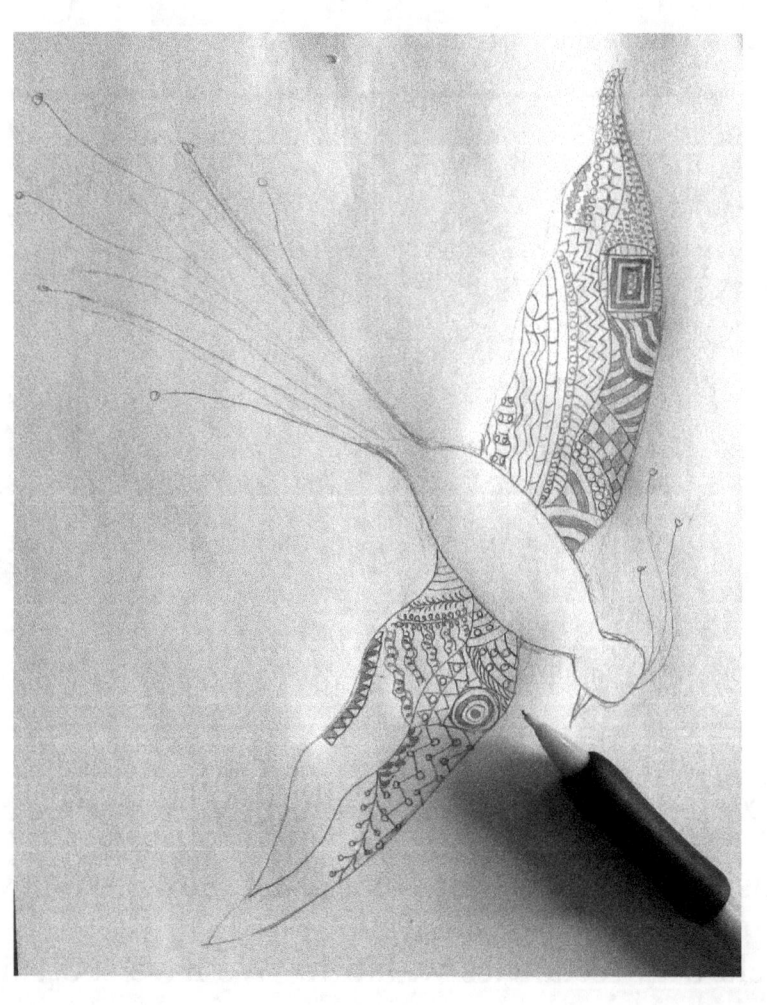

We have used more waves, circles and rays to finish off the right wing. We have also given our bird an eye. Can you find the flowers we put there?

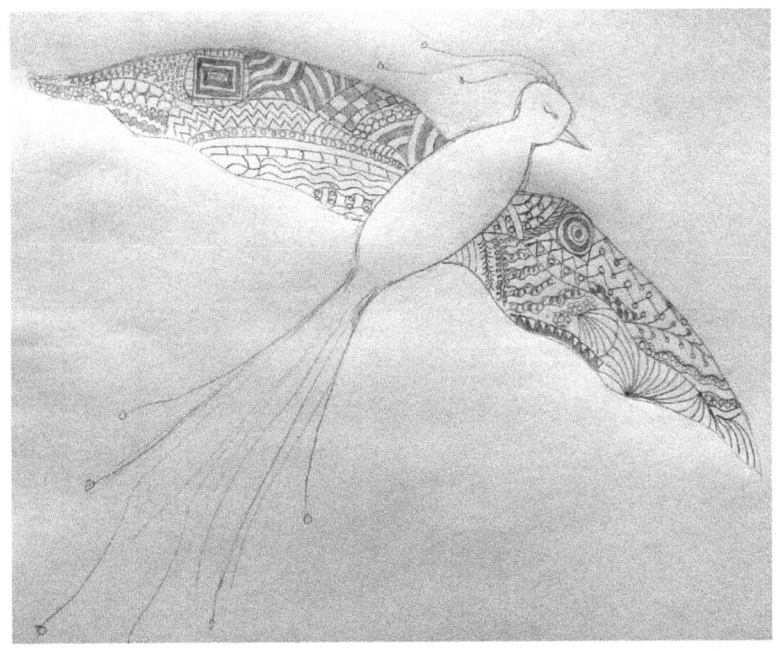

Chapter 6: The Bear

We've done a bird. Now, we are going to finish the book instructing you on how to draw something a little more involved, a bear. You will be walked through how to draw the bear in the first few steps. After, you will be shown how to fill it in. If you already know how to draw a bear, a simple bear on all fours like the one below is what we will be working with for the final exercise.

Start out with a curve:

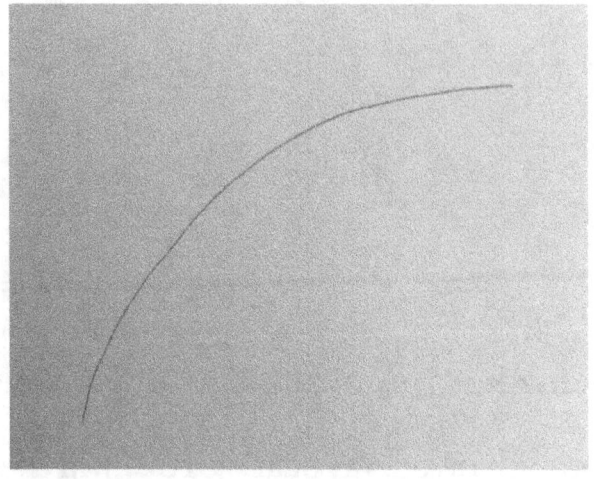

Now, draw a line for the head. This will give our bear

a little direction.

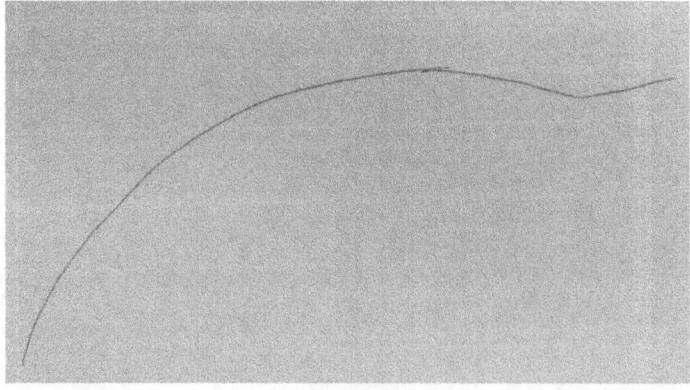

Now, we're going to draw a rounder curve for the
bear's rear. Bring the curve down and around:

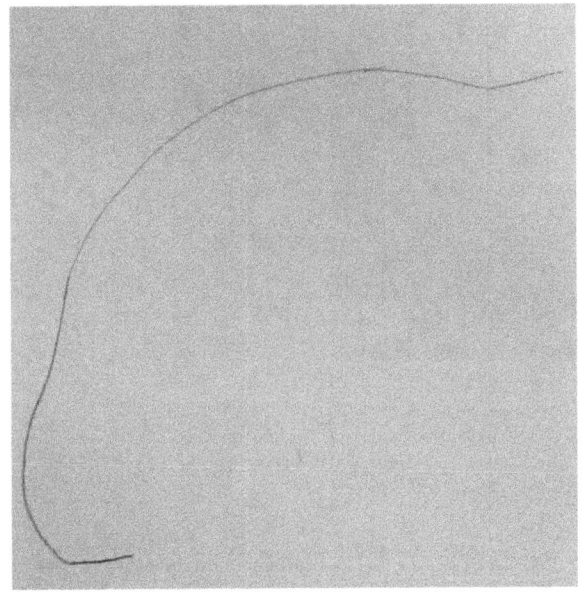

Now, we're adding a little to the head area. Little by
little, he is beginning to take shape. Your drawing
should be looking like this:

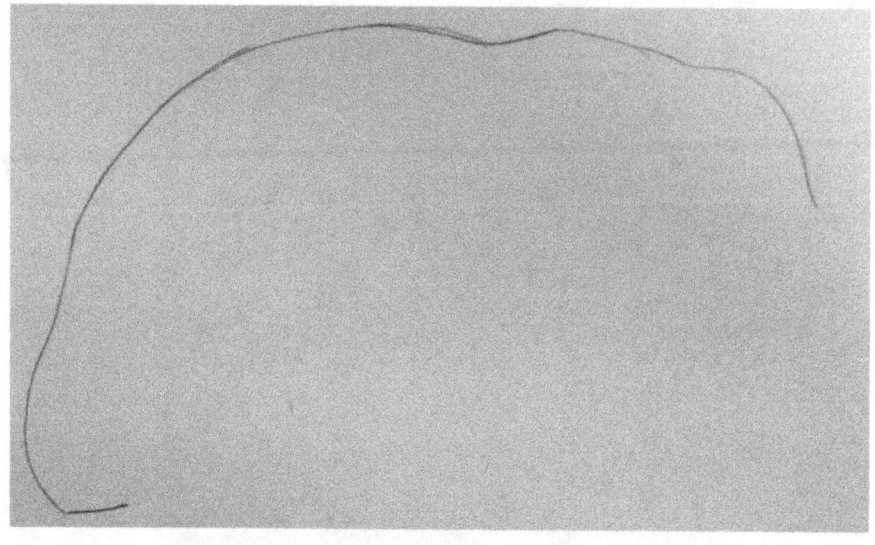

Now, let's go back to the rear and add a few more

curves for the foot and hind quarter.

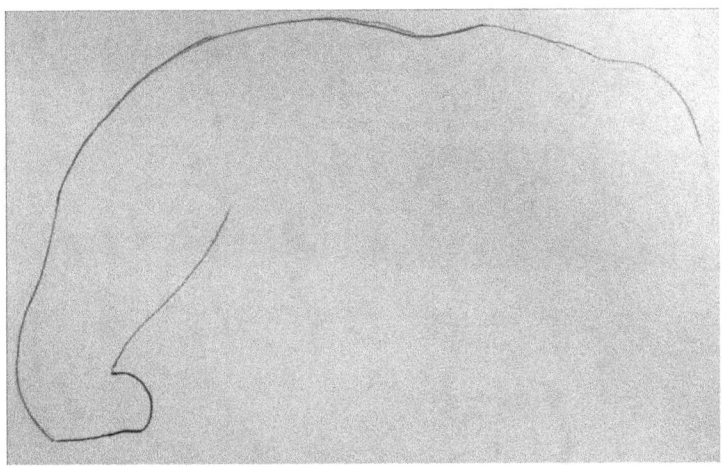

Give him a belly by drawing another smooth curve underneath.

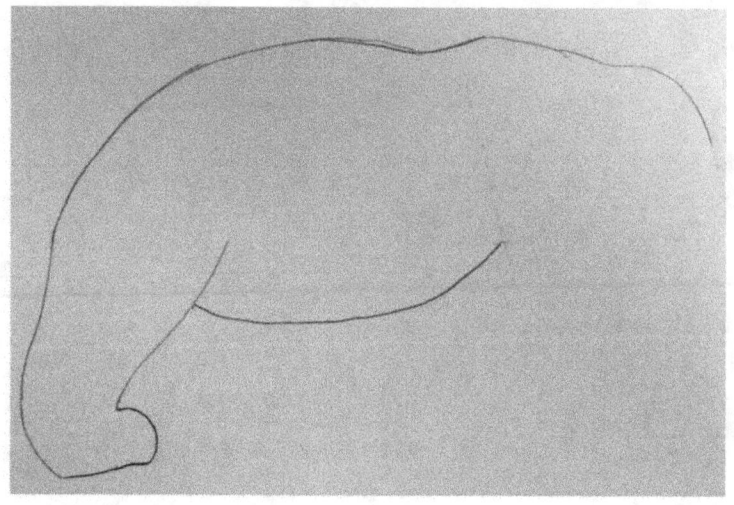

Draw another line to give him a front leg and to start on the front quarter.

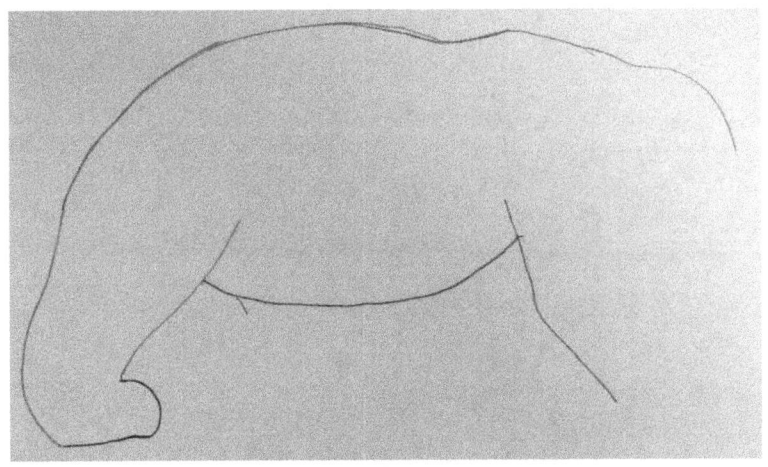

Our bear needs another rear leg. We have to give him

a little depth and make him look like he is getting

ready walk instead of just being flat.

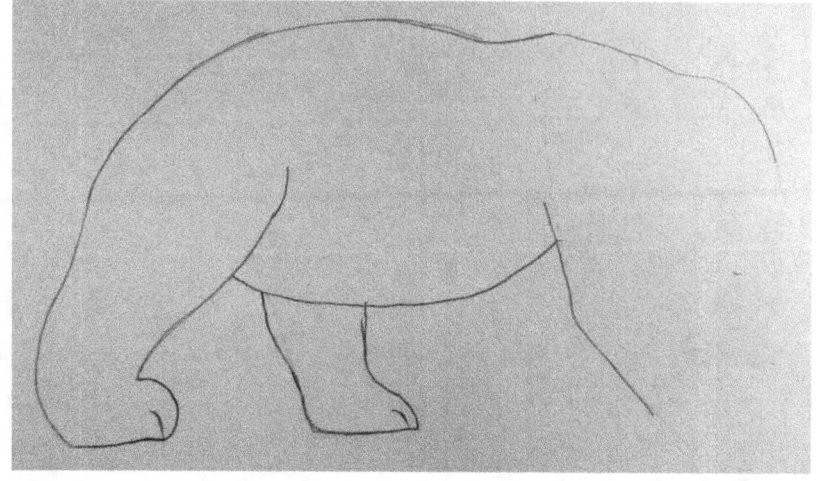

Let's add a rear front leg and finish off the leg that is closest to us. Now, add a couple more curves to start defining the head, as you see here:

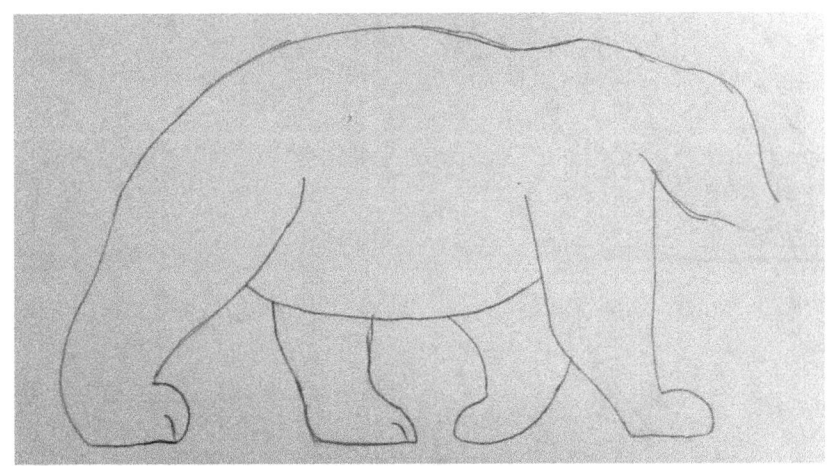

Let's finish off his head, add ears and a mouth. He's a happy little bear. You can go back later and take out some lines, but for now, we're focusing on getting him finished before we start on adding the patterns. He's still missing something.

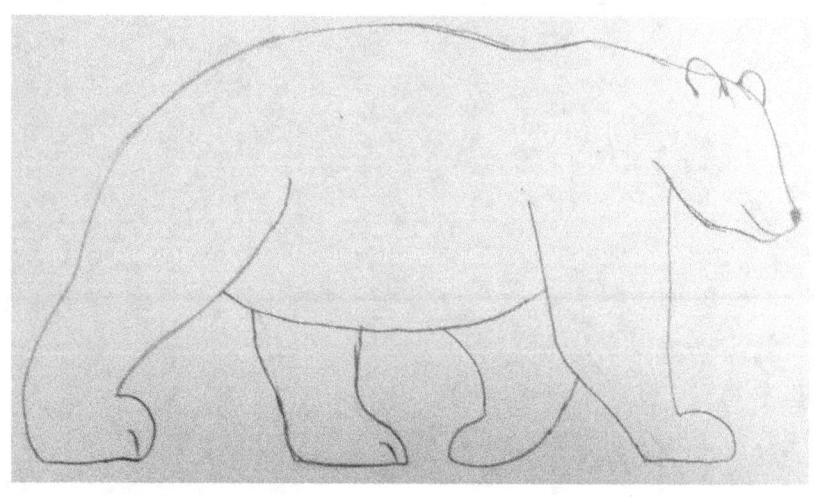

There we go. Now, it looks like he is up to something.

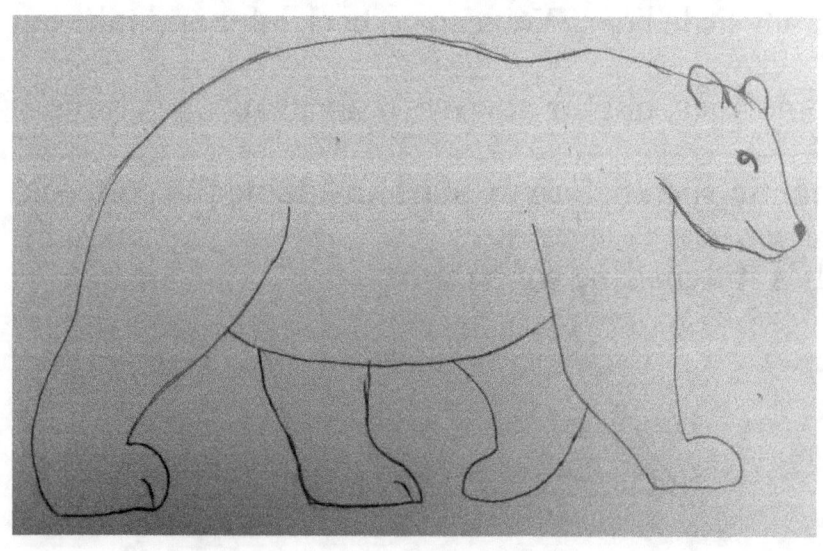

To start filling him in, we are drawing some semi-circles and some curved lines along the contour of his rear end.

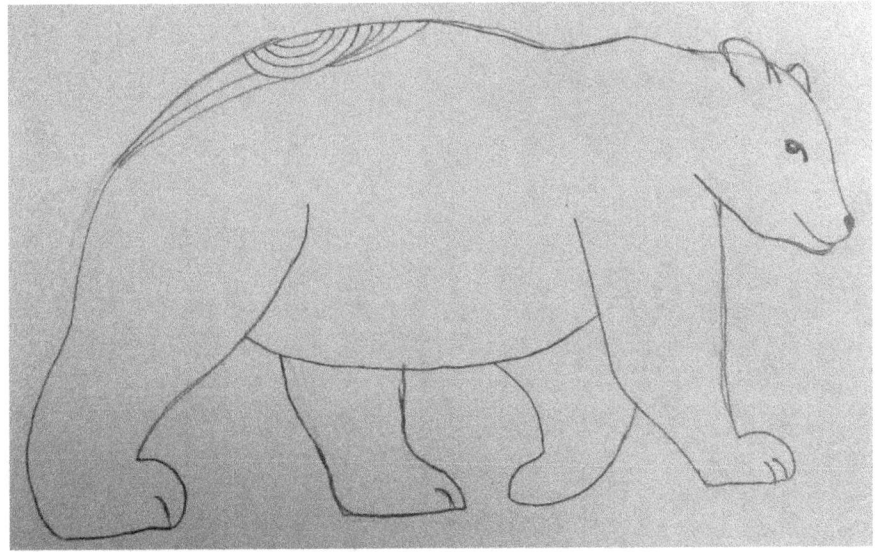

Adding some more semi-circles and a few long waves on the haunch will let help get the piece going. We're going to work from the rear to the front. This will give us direction and will help with the flow of the composition.

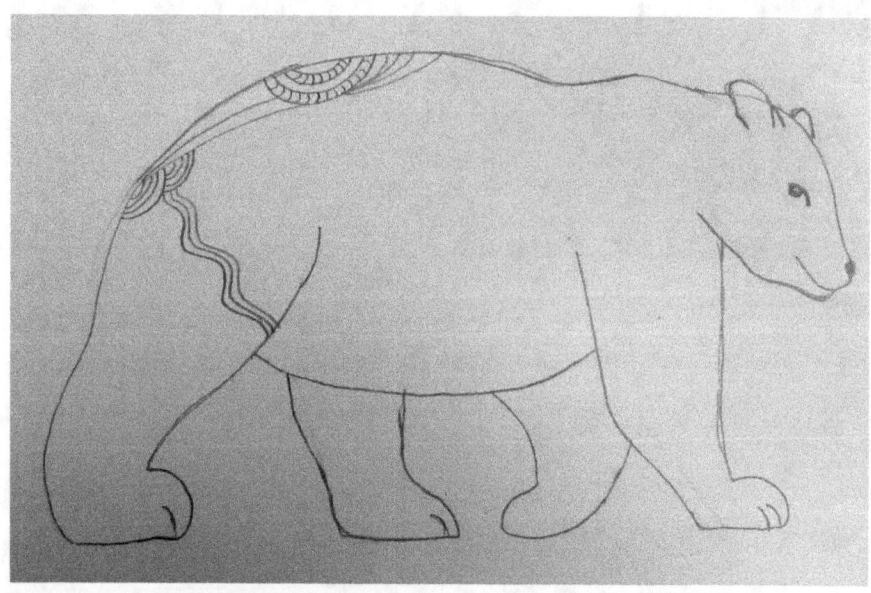

You can pull from previous exercises to give our bear more patterns and make him look really nice. Here, we have started drawing the paisley tear, and we have added a couple of rays, a little wider apart. We have also added lines to the rays instead of shading them. We have also filled in some of the semi-circles on his back.

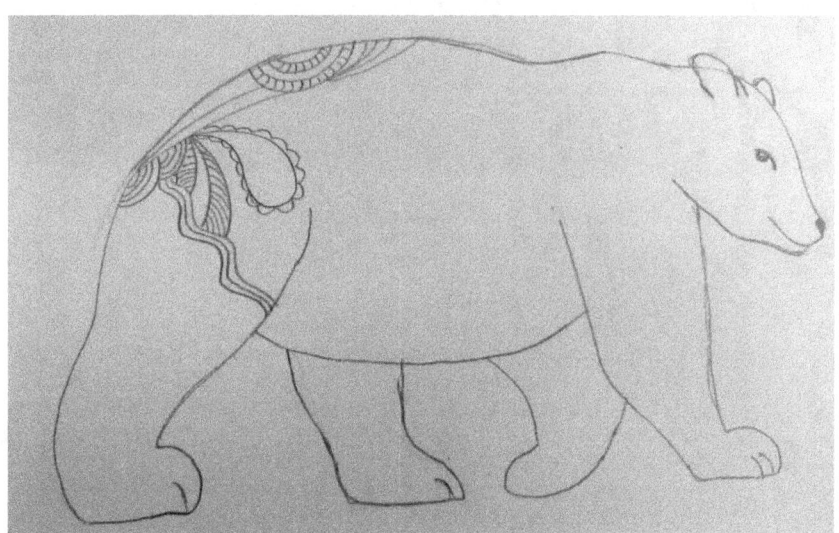

Fill in the paisley tear before we move on to the next part. See how we added petals to the tear? We're going to do a little more to it.

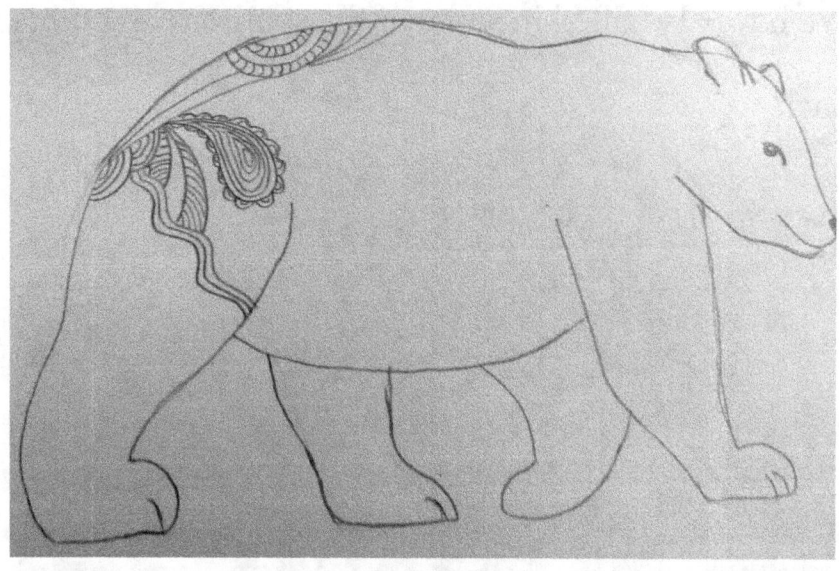

Put in some circles, and rays going in different directions. We have drawn some curves the go along the contour of his hind quarter. We added a final layer to the tear and shaded some of the drops inside.

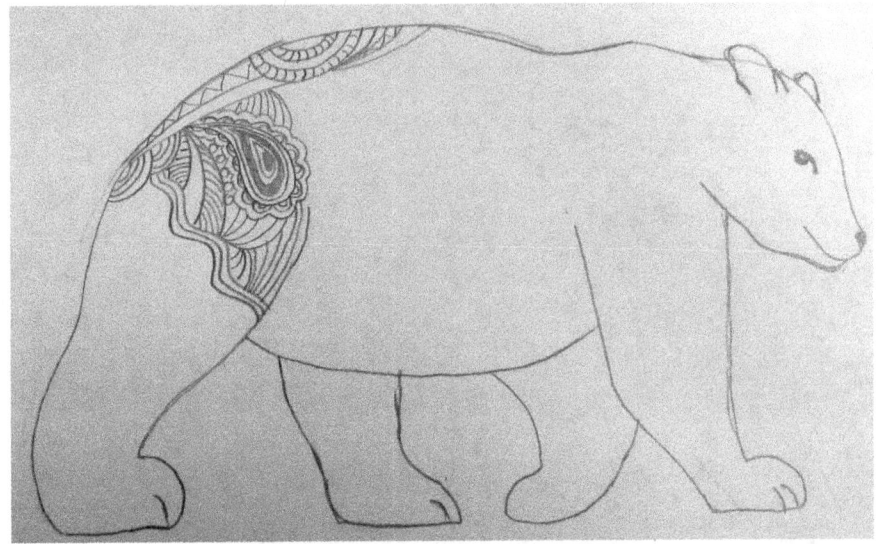

Let's have a little fun. Add candy striping by shading in one of the rays. Now, draw triangles in another, and waves and shaded circles in yet two more. Look closely before moving to the next step to make sure you haven't missed anything.

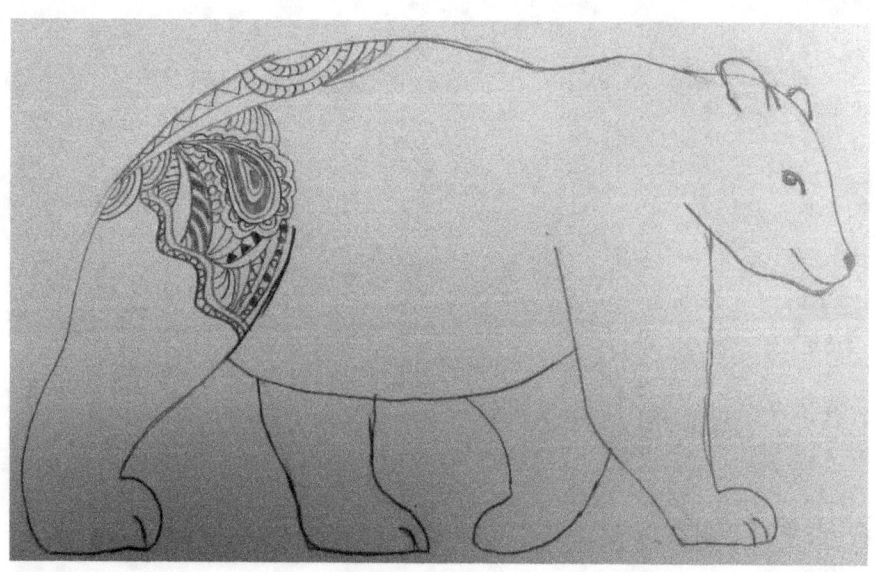

Add a few more diamonds and circles to the back of our bear.

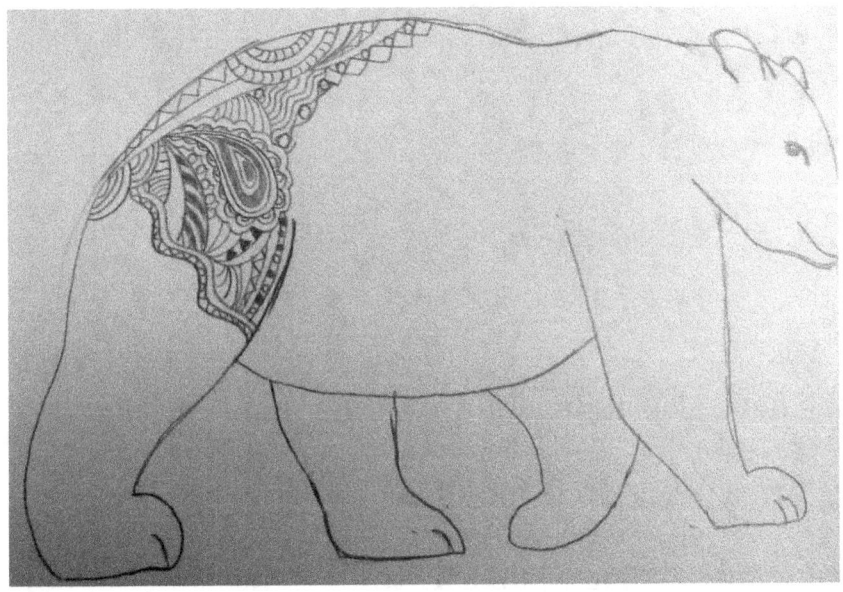

In this picture, we have added semi-circles and shaded them:

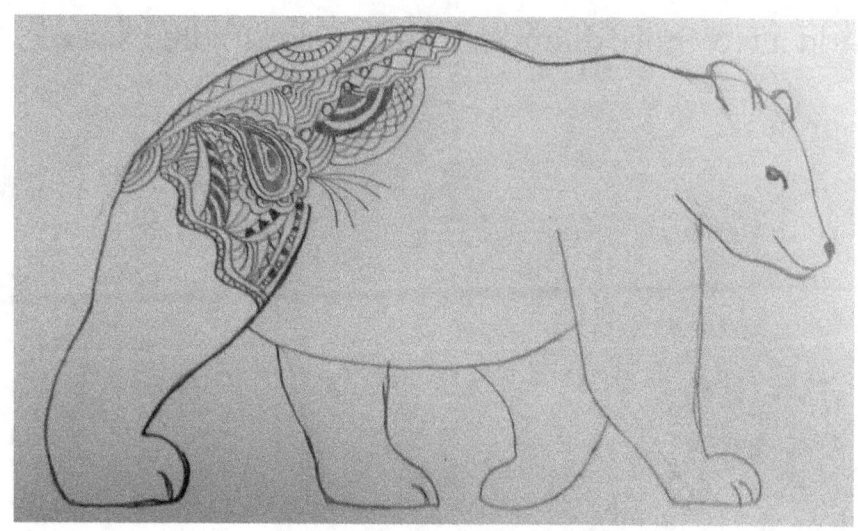

We have also added bumps to the semi-circles and drawn a semi-circle for an edge. We have also drawn some rays that are pointing toward the center of our bear.

In case the rays as seen here. Now, draw a few more heading back toward the haunch of our bear. We've also added some lined patterns where our abstract fan is and included alternating shaded circles within another ray. See how everything is coming together and flowing nicely.

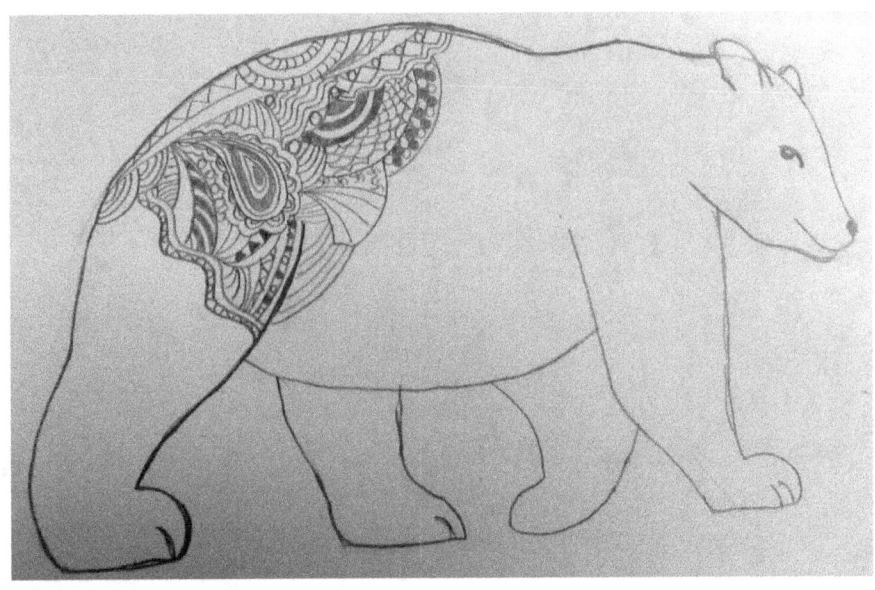

Let's focus back on the leg. Fan out, heading down by drawing loops. Now, add some rays and curves. Hop down to the foot and add a flower. Take the time to darken the main lines of the bear to set them apart. This will give you a better point of reference.

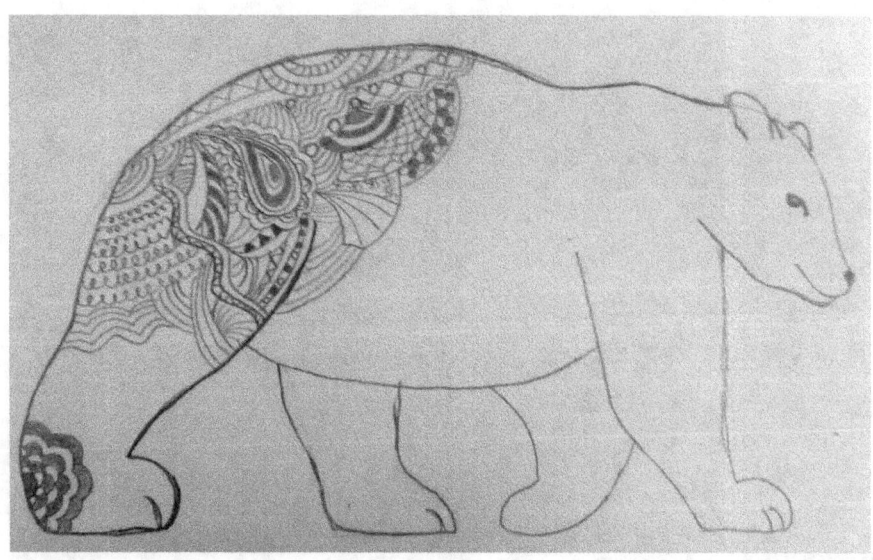

We're going to get a little fancy with this part. Draw rays from the waves and fill them in as you see below. Now, add some curves, shading two and placing circles in the center of them. You are now going to connect the leg by adding a few more curves. Use shading to give the other curves depth, and go back to the back and add lines to the fans. Now, add a few more curves up top and fill a couple in with wavy lines. He's looking good.

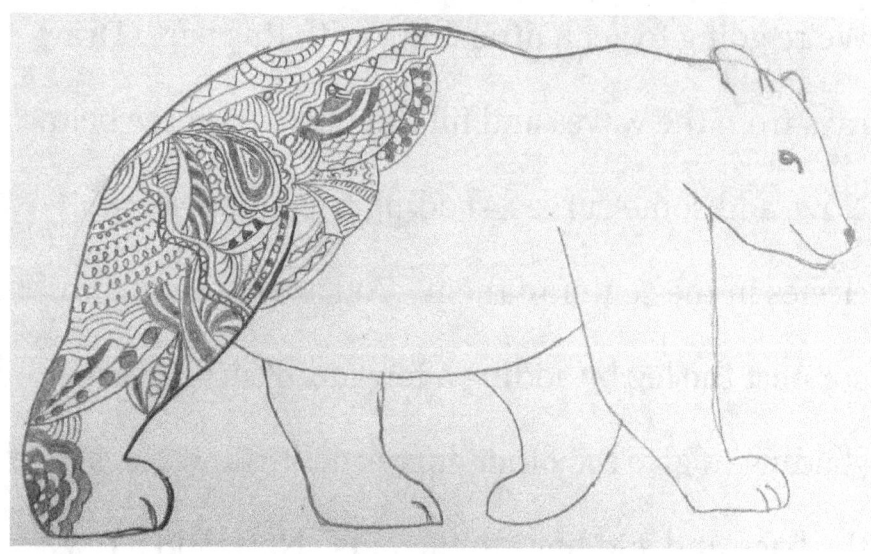

In order to finish the front hind quarter, we add
circles encased in a wave, a few more wavy lines-two
of which have lines, and wavy rays jutting out from
the flower to the rest of the paw. Can you spot any
other differences?

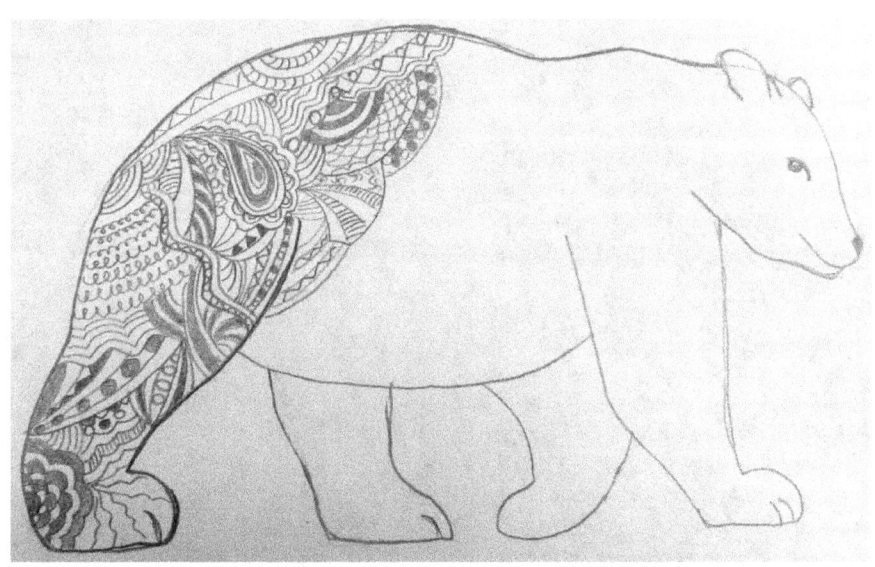

Just a little bit to the right of the main pattern, place a four-pointed star. Then, draw lines like the ones you see in the picture below.

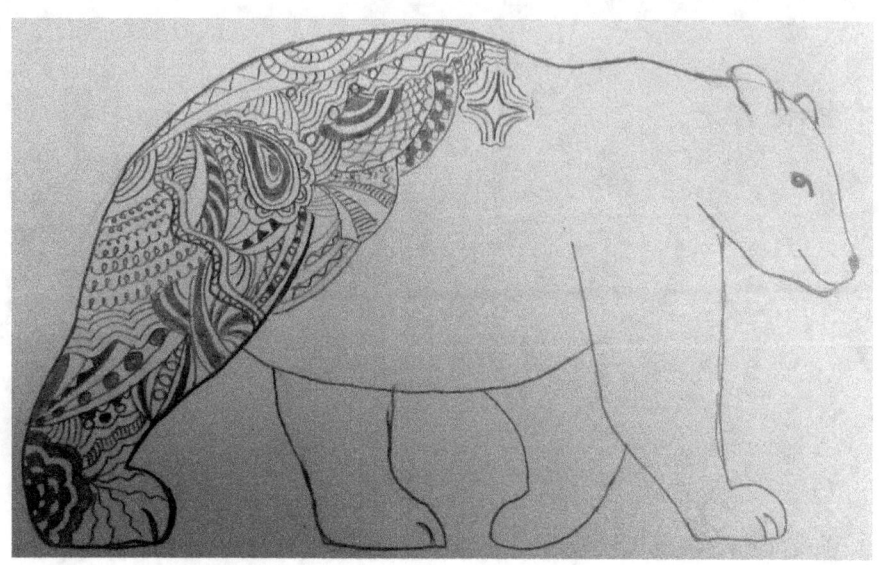

To continue, make rays going from about an inch from the main pattern towards it. Now draw some more in the opposite direction. Accentuate with wavy lines, and then add shaded circles to the outside of the wavy lines. Slightly below the star, draw a few arrowheads, shade every other one in, and then draw bumps, ending them with small circles in the indentations. Draw a small bumpy line on the bottom outside edge of the star. We have also filled in the star.

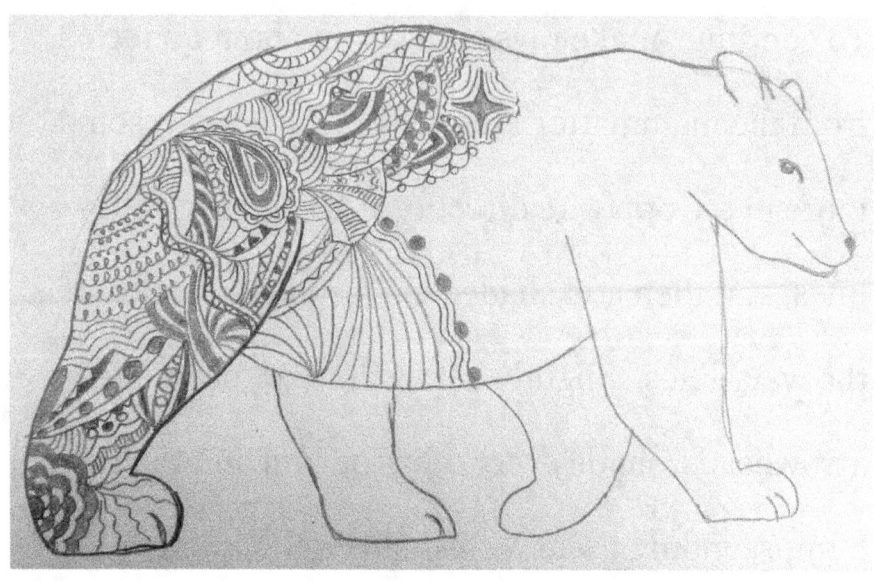

We add a little more character to the piece, we are going to add a few more bumpy lines above the shaded circles as the picture below shows:

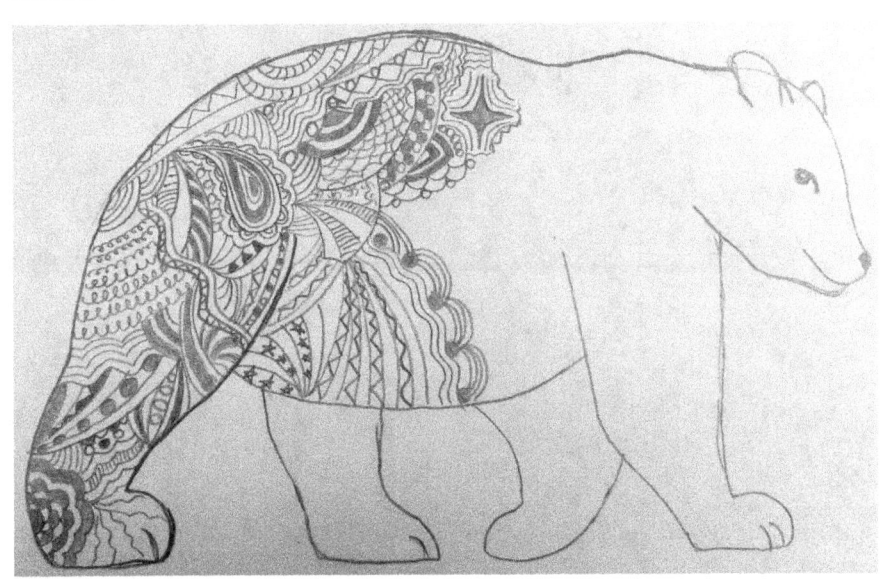

Here, we have added a circle and decorated it with bumps, shaded it and also provided more waves and curves.

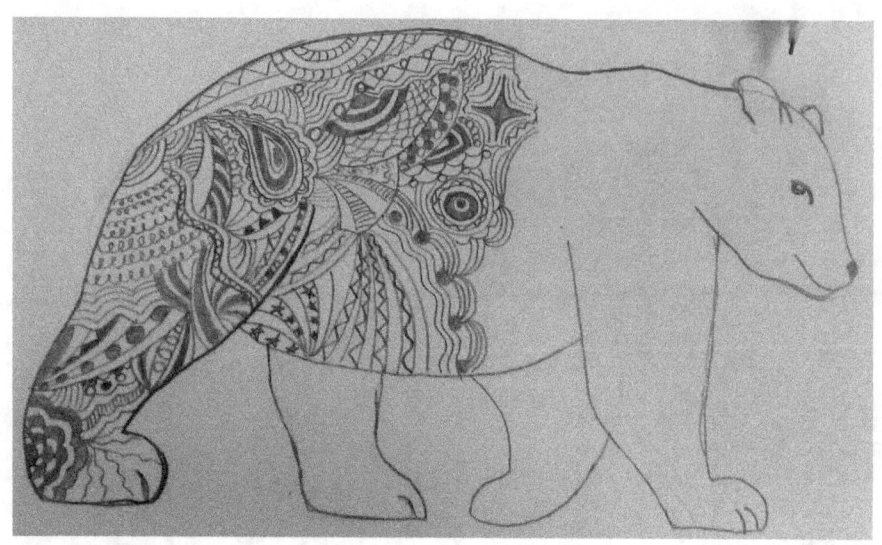

This is the circle close-up so you can see all the details. We see now that it looks more like a swirl. We have drawn more curves on the left side and bumps on the outside as well as a wavy line in the circle itself.

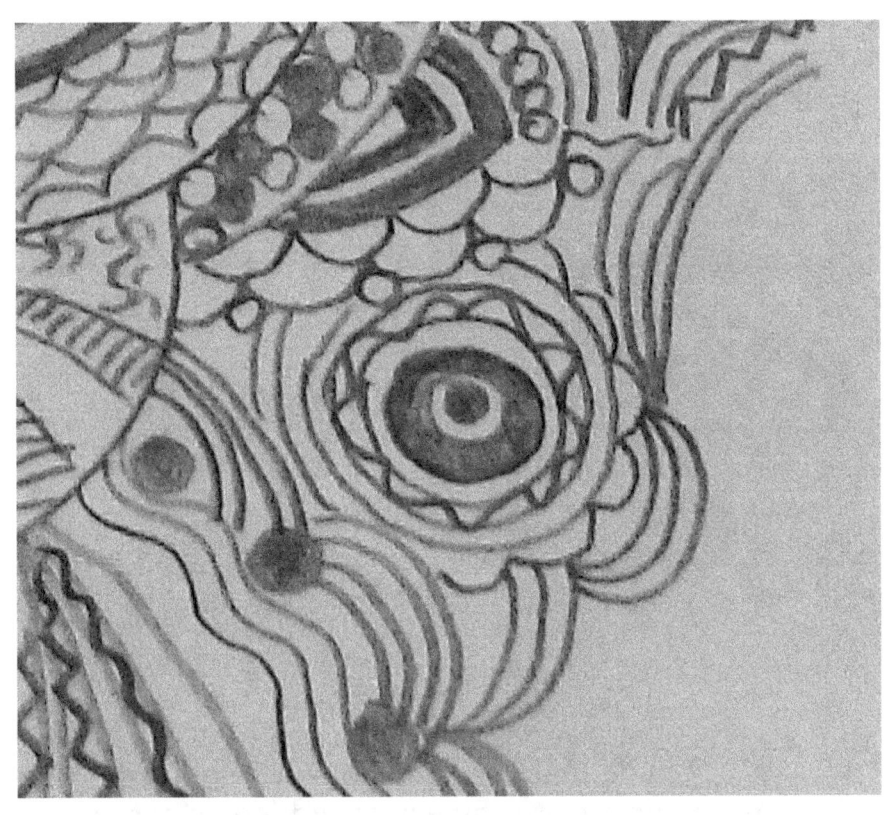

Draw radiating wavy lines going toward the front

quarter:

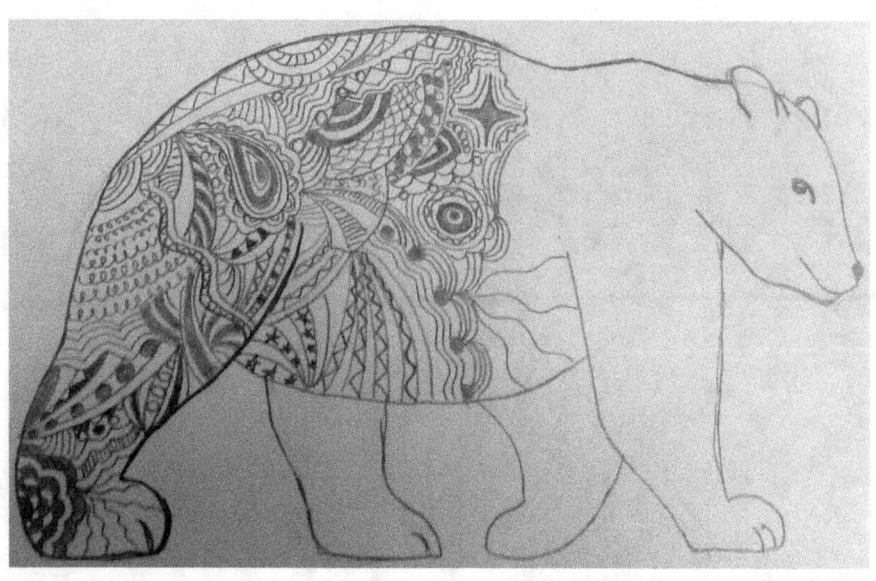

We've added bumps to the waves, added curves, a feather shape and another flower on the end of the feather shape.

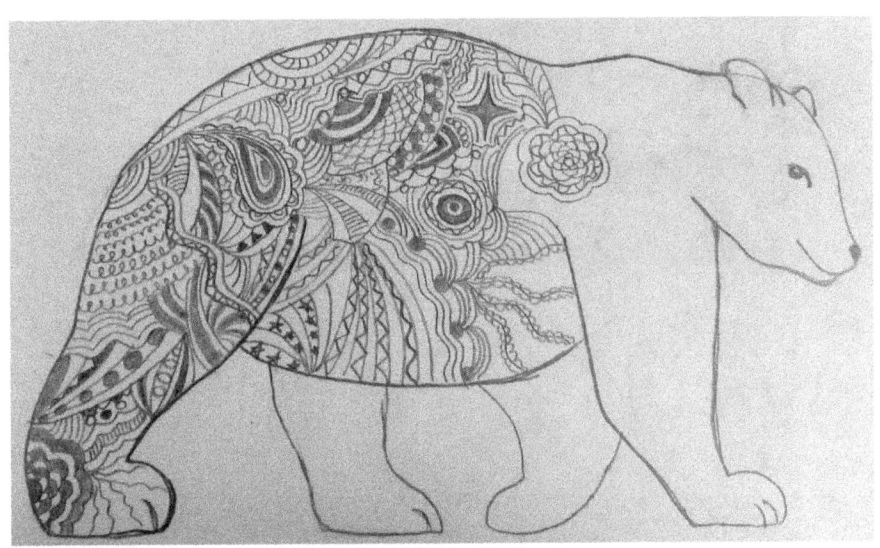

Let's see all the detail in the flower close-up:

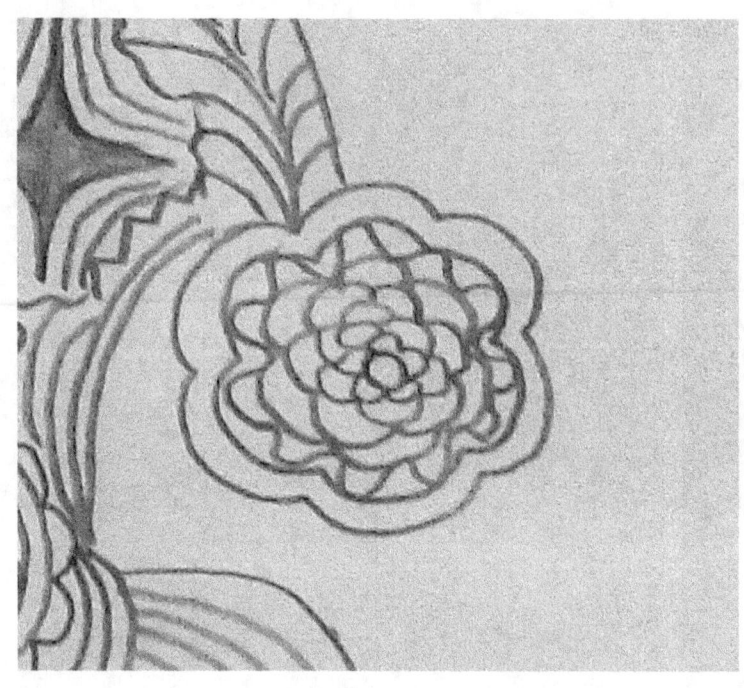

We started with the flower shape in a previous chapter and added waves and then framed it with bigger petals.

Let's stay in this area for a bit. We can make this part more eye-catching by adding shaded rays as below:

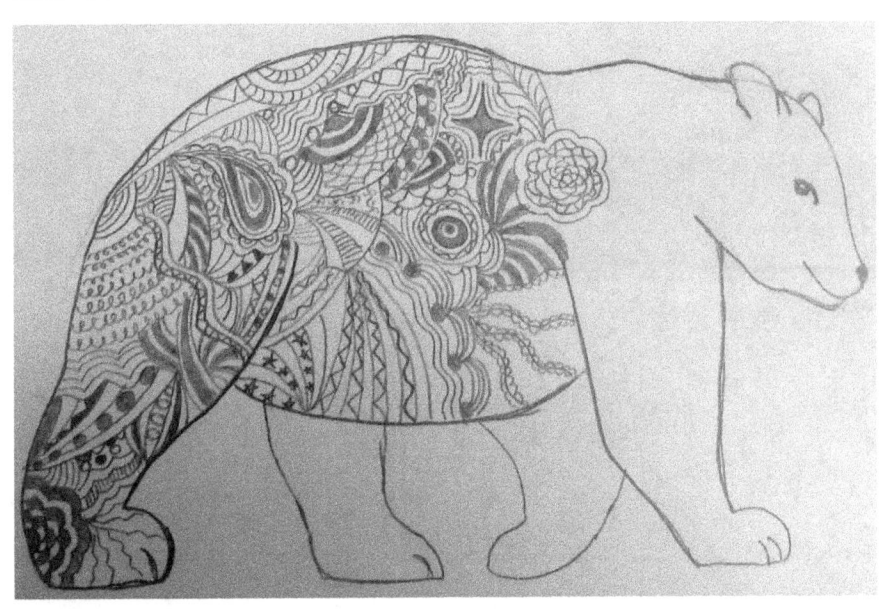

Moving on to the front paw, we first start by drawing two wavy lines and then a series of connected loops. The next picture is going to have a lot more detail, but I will walk you through it.

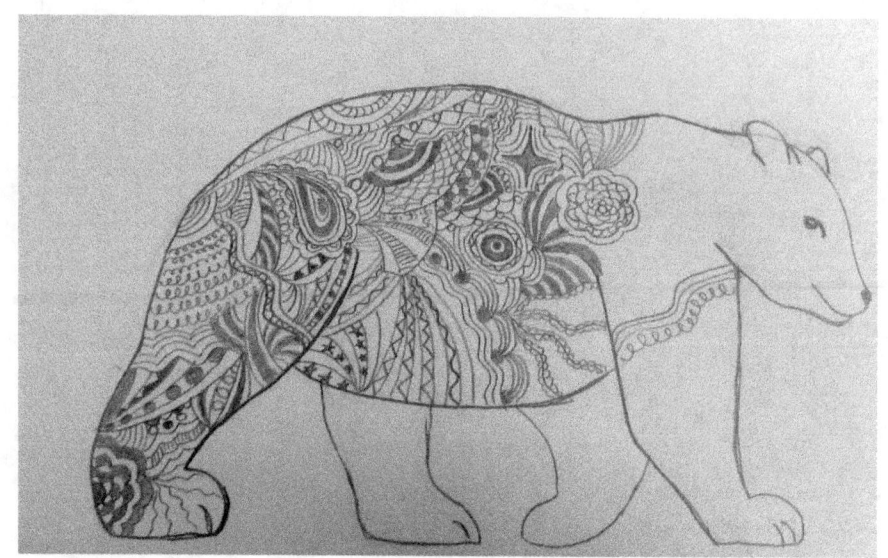

We have now drawn the attention to the front paw by adding shaded rays that shoot out from the dot under the loopy line. We have also added shaded waves. Above the waves on the leg, we have more curves, waves and dots. In the middle of the larger shaded rays, we have drawn curves with circles within them that stop at the foot. The foot contains more wavy lines, some shaded and one with shaded hash marks. We have also started defining the neck area.

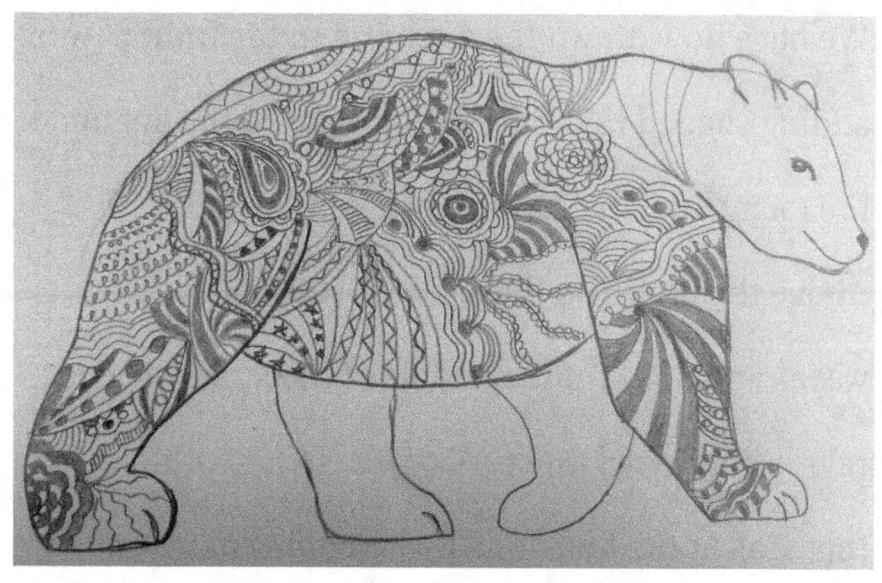

Since we are focusing on the neck, here is that section of the composition. Take note how the design contours to the neck and allows it define where the neck begins and ends. Just fill in this section as you see it in the picture.

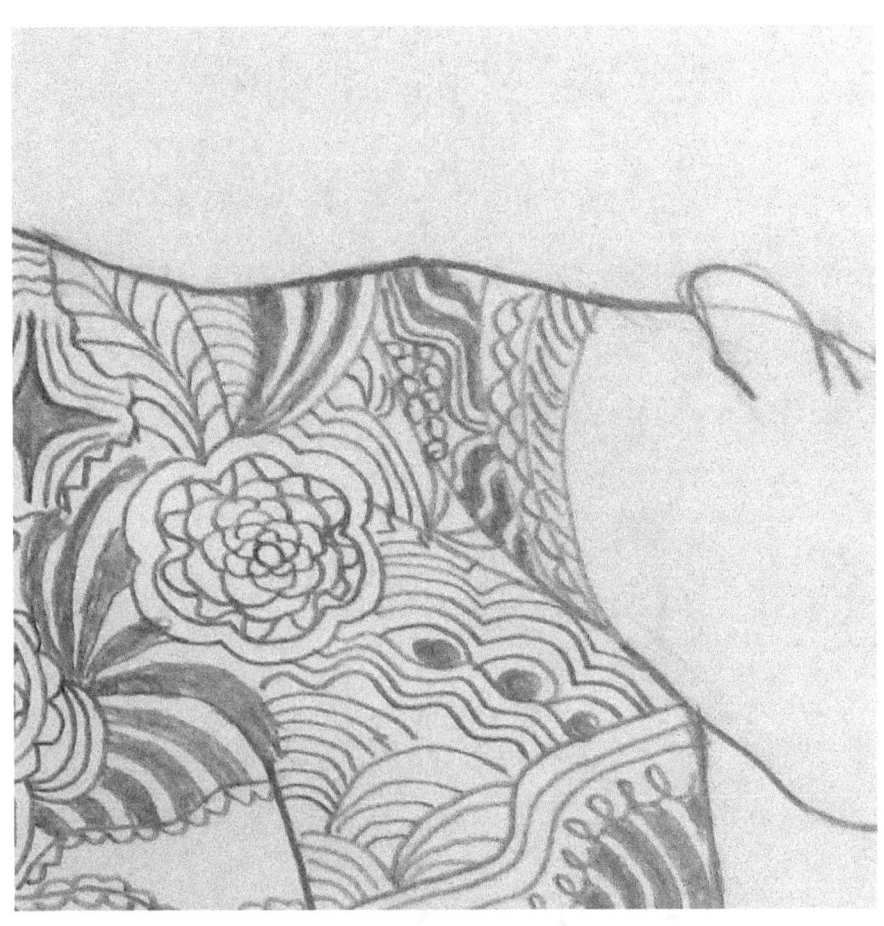

The next few pictures are going to focus on the legs

in the rear of the composition.

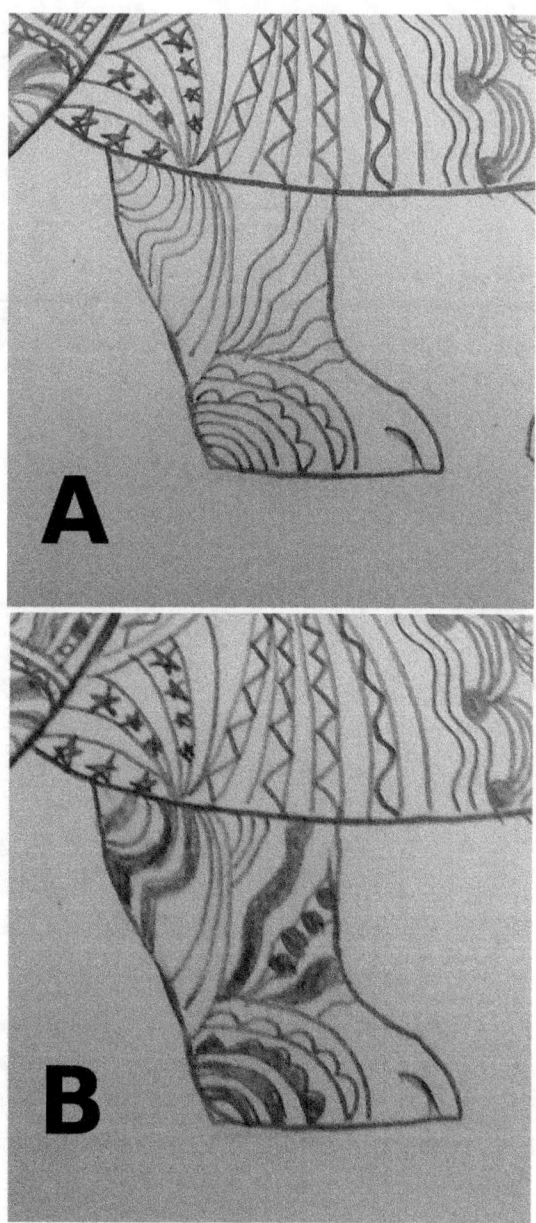

A. We have filled in the back rear leg with the detailing you see here. We have left the front part of the paw plain, but, when we finish, it won't really matter.

B. We have added circles in the detailing as well as shaded in some areas to make the lines more prevalent. Even though we didn't add patterns to the toe area, the details we did use sets it apart so you can see the front of the foot.

This is the front-rear leg of the bear. We have added the details you see in the picture. The curves are adding contour and the shaded areas highlight the rear paw.

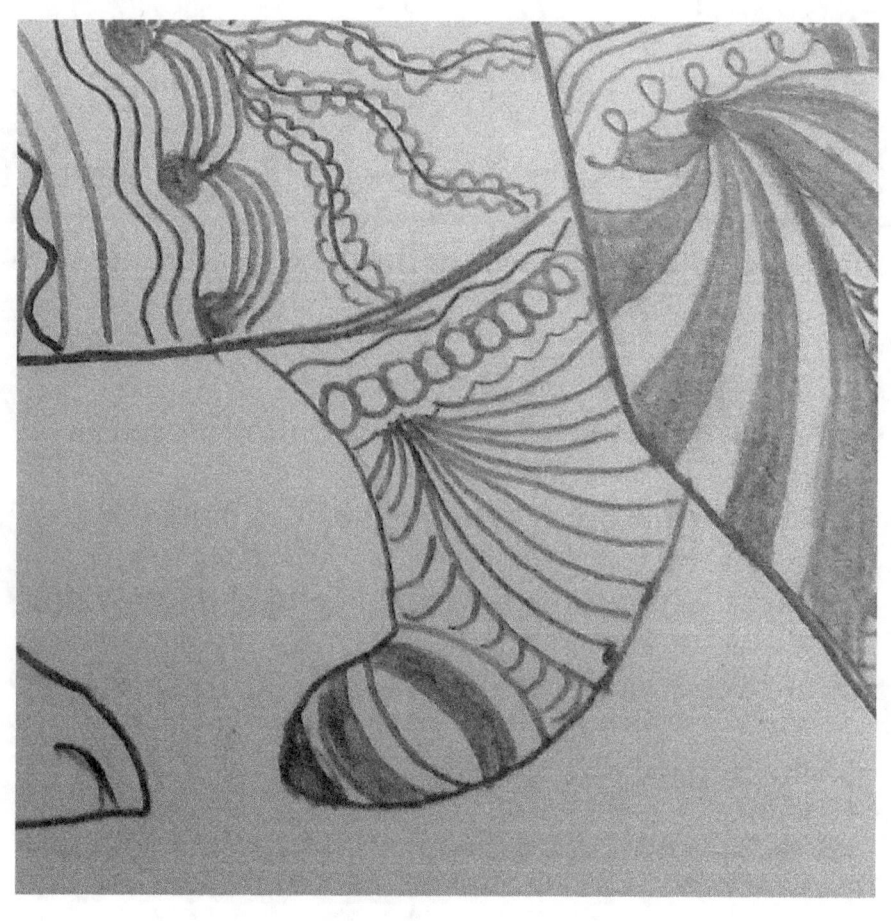

This is our finished bear:

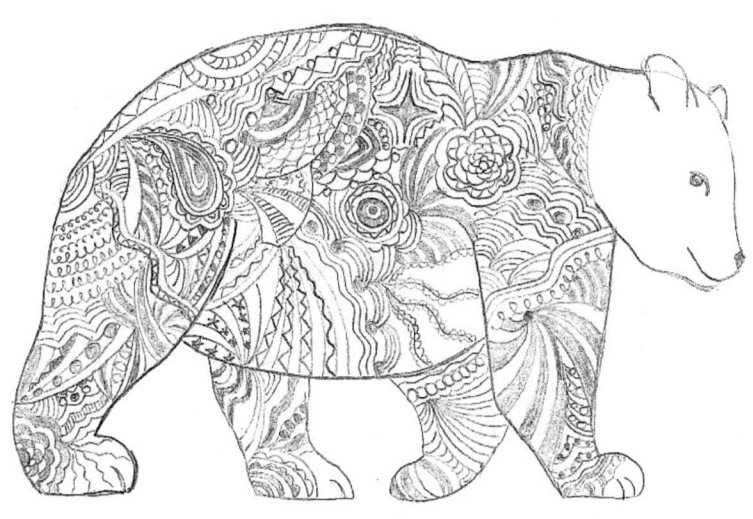

To make the frame of the bear stand out, go back over it with a soft pencil or black pen. You can also go back over some of the details as well. We see the complete composition in the picture even though we have filled in the frame with what most people would call scribbles or doodles. Each was placed to accentuate the composition and further give the person looking at the finished piece an idea of the shape of the frame. The patterns in the frame also help to highlight certain parts of the composition, adding to the pieces as a whole and not taking anything away from it.

Conclusion

There is no right or wrong way for drawing zendoodle pictures. "Zen", the first three words of this type of art form is the practice of visualizing what you want to achieve before you achieve it. It is a nod to the Zen monks who have spent millennia perfecting their talents. "Tangle" is in reference to the patterns within the frame itself. They have no certain order of appearance. This mean you can put as much or as little detail in your work as you wish.

Before you start to fill in your frame, close your eyes, and take a deep breath. Let it out slowly and picture, in your mind how you want the piece to look like when you are finished. How you want it to be contoured, shaded, and if or how you want to incorporate smaller frames into the piece to make it stand out. Visualize yourself drawing the frame and filling it in. Look at the finished work in your mind and make any changes you feel need to be changed. Once you are happy with the piece of art in your mind, you are ready to fill in your frame physically.

If you feel that you are not ready, or good enough to draw the more complex frames. There are duty free images you can print off of the internet to get you started. You can also buy tracing paper and trace the frame from a book or magazine. Don't think because you are not comfortable drawing the frame, that you can't make a composition. After you have traced pictures to use as frames, your hand will have memorized them through practice, and you will be able to replicate any image you wish to use.

I hope this book has helped you gain a new understanding about this new and emerging art form. I encourage you to try the exercises in this book, and then go out and find your own inspiration for creating these wonderful and relaxing pieces of meditative art.

Now, grab your paper, and pencil. Find a quiet spot to be alone with your thoughts and let your mind do all the work.

www.ingramcontent.com/pod-product-compliance
Lightning Source LLC
Chambersburg PA
CBHW070325190526
45169CB00005B/1745